elegant MACHINE QUILTING

JOANIE ZEIER POOLE

©2005 Joanie Zeier Poole

Published by

kp books
An Imprint of F+W Publications

700 East State Street • Iola, WI 54990-0001
715-445-2214 • 888-457-2873

Our toll-free number to place an order or obtain
a free catalog is (800) 258-0929.

Library of Congress Catalog Number: 2004113672

ISBN: 0-87349-898-4

Designed by Donna Mummery

Edited by Susan Sliwicki and Nicole Gould

Printed in the United States of America

Dedication

I dedicate this book to:

- My parents, for teaching me the satisfaction of hard work.
- Harriet Hargrave, for inventing this art form, and Diane Gaudynski, for sharing her expertise and teaching heirloom machine quilting to me.
- Bob, my partner in love and life.
- Our boys, Ben and Aaron: May my work inspire you to follow your dreams.
- The readers of this book: Honor your talents with time for mastering this skill.

Acknowledgments

I would like to thank Hobbs Bonded Fibers, Superior Threads, YLI Corp. and RJR Fabrics for their support with their products.

I also wish to thank my teachers, friends and family, who encouraged me with their support in making this dream a reality.

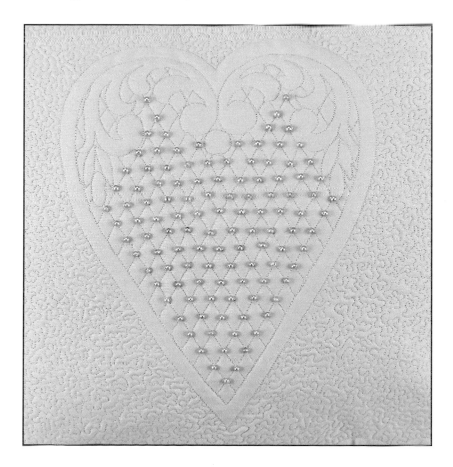

Contents

Introduction

Words of Motivation

From the first seeds of inspiration to the selection of quilting designs, fabrics and patterns, right through the final stitching, every step of quilt making is so much fun!

I love the fact that "quilting" includes such a vast array of techniques that you could spend a lifetime working and never explore all the possibilities. I love that after so many years, after so many quilts, I still can start over with a new skill to master, as was the case when I learned about heirloom machine quilting a few years ago.

If you are new to machine quilting or perhaps trying free-motion designs for the first time, I encourage you to embrace it as a skill that increases your ability to get projects finished, have greater satisfaction in your work and show off your creative abilities.

Over the years, I tried my hand at machine quilting. Like many others, I kept myself chained to my walking foot, the training wheels of machine quilting, using it for straight-line quilting only. My life took a wonderful new direction in February 2000, when I learned heirloom machine quilting from Diane Gaudynski. It was after spending three days at one of Diane's workshops that I realized the quilts of my dreams now were possible!

I personally am saddened by the recent trend to produce patchwork tops that the makers do not intend to finish themselves, but rather send out to be quilted. Others who never have tried to machine quilt on their home machines are considering purchasing long-arm quilting machines. I know that I never could give up experiencing the joy and satisfaction of having one of my pieced tops become a quilt right before my eyes. I encourage you to try machine quilting on the machine you already have and experience that satisfaction for yourself.

I hope that you will find encouragement in the fact that I never used to be good at sewing with a machine. Until recently, all of my best work had been done by hand —embroidery, appliqué and prized hand quilting. I always have been able to draw, and I have a good sense of color and proportion. I can conceptualize my thoughts into the necessary processes needed to design my own patterns. But who would have guessed that I would have to conquer my greatest weakness to achieve this skill? Until I learned heirloom machine quilting, the elaborate quilting designs that I loved were locked in my dreams.

Thanks to heirloom machine quilting, those designs have found their way out of my dreams and onto the pages of this book. I hope that my artwork speaks to your heart and touches your life enough to encourage you to create these beautiful, little projects. I hope my joy of bringing these designs to you is apparent in this work and that these designs will provide you with many hours of enjoyable stitching and wonderful treasures to share with your loved ones.

At first glance, the quilting designs may look complex. Try one to discover for yourself how simple elegant machine quilting really is. Get out a square of solid-colored fabric, trace your favorite pattern and give it a try. Relax, then start with a positive outlook and a small project to test the technique. Who couldn't spare one square?

With practice comes confidence. Your efforts will improve with every attempt. If you have the desire, and if you continue to practice, you, too, will find the key to unlock the part of your brain that holds you back. I challenge you to produce beautiful works of art that show your spirit.

Think of your quilting as an expression of your talents. Use the same care in your machine quilting that you would to achieve a fine hand-quilted piece. Follow your intuition and stretch your color palette or design choices. Be brave, be bold, and be creative! Enjoy each step in the process, celebrate your achievements and delight in your progress. Include others in your journey and share the gifts you possess. You will be richly rewarded. It is with great joy and enthusiasm that I present this first book of designs to you.

Enjoy your quilting!

Joanie

How to Use This Book

Tips

Learn new approaches and avoid potential problems with these bits of helpful information.

Quilting Sequence and Starting Arrows

Because this is a how-to book, I give information about the logical order to follow when stitching each design. The Start Here arrow on the pattern will indicate where to place your needle to begin. Follow each plan to have the fewest starts and stops necessary.

Pattern Pullout Sheets

Full-size designs appear in the pattern pullout in the back of the book.

Transfer the designs from the pattern insert to a convenient size for easy handling rather than trying to trace the designs from the large sheets of paper onto the fabric. Some large designs only show one-half of the mirror-image design; those designs will need to be copied or traced to create the full-size image. Dotted lines indicate the center of the design; use them to match the sections of the complete design.

Use a fine-line permanent marker to trace the outlines by hand, or make copies with a copy machine. If the design area is larger than the copier, simply copy several sections of the design and tape them together to make a complete design. See Basic Techniques for more information about transferring designs.

tip

Most printers for home computers will print on 8½" x 14" paper as well as the standard 8½" x 11" size. Those few added inches may give you the extra space you need for a pattern.

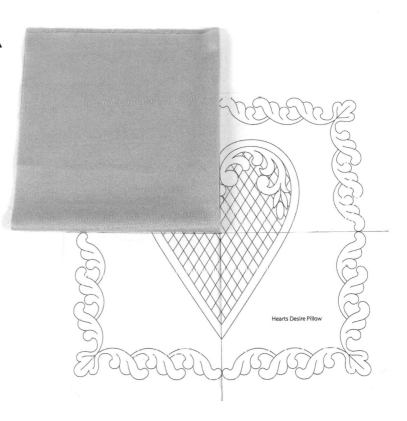

Hearts Desire Pillow

Getting Started

Learn the **basics** of heirloom machine quilting,
including how to set up your sewing area, **choosing** the
right **tools** for the job, and what machine and incidental
supplies to have on hand before you **begin**.

Getting Started

Frequently Asked Questions About Machine Quilting

What is heirloom machine quilting? Machine quilting, which includes straight-line and free-motion quilting, can be accomplished by using either your home sewing machine or a large, commercial machine. Heirloom machine quilting is performed on a regular home machine, using advanced free-motion techniques. The scale of the work is refined to produce a decorative, sculptured quilt surface. As the name implies, this technique is based on the look of the traditional heirloom quilts, yet differs significantly because those beautiful older sisters usually were quilted entirely by hand.

What is fueling the current popularity of machine quilting? There is a huge interest in quilting, with 21 million quilters in the United States alone, according to a survey published by Quilter's Newsletter Magazine. Designers and manufacturers of fabrics and patterns are offering many beautiful supplies. We have the desire to make more quilts, and quilting them by machine gets the process completed quickly. With these techniques, you can complete your projects at home, on the sewing machine you already own, in a fraction of the time it would take to quilt the same piece by hand.

Joanie, why do you love heirloom machine quilting? I always have had the dream of making quilts with elegant and complicated quilting designs. Since I learned this technique, I can stitch more impressive designs, and I have the satisfaction of getting the work done quickly! I can create designs that would not be possible with hand quilting in the amount of time I have to invest in the project. Now I just draw the intricate patterns on my quilt top, and focus on a small area to fill with wonderful images.

Is heirloom machine quilting hard to do? No. Even though it may look like it is tough, let me fill you in on a little secret. It looks so much more difficult that it really is.

Consider a simple quilting design that you assume would be easy, a design with one, lonely object on an empty field. If the stitching is off the line, the mistake is very noticeable, because there is nothing else to distract your eye. With an intricate design surrounded by background fillers, there is so much to look at that the mistake may never be seen.

Machine quilters have been told that they should use only continuous-line designs. I agree that it is best to have the least number of starting and stopping points possible. However, when the design includes a stippled background around the motifs, one isolated motif can be connected to another without cutting the thread and simply stippling a path to it.

Necessities, Supplies and Tools of the Trade

Purchase the best supplies that you can afford. Honor your time and effort in all stages of the process with quality tools; your work is worth the investment.

I made this list of recommended supplies and tools because of the success I have found when using them. These are not the only options available; others may work as well or better for you. I am always on the lookout for new tools that make this process better, and manufacturers are coming up with new gadgets every day.

The Sewing Machine

Heirloom machine quilting does not require a fancy computerized sewing machine or extensive attachments. The skill of the quilter is as important as a well-conditioned sewing machine and trial tests with suggested supplies. Confidence builds with practice and makes a machine quilter successful. While some of the features on the new machines are very handy, the only function you really need to do heirloom quilting on your machine is for the needle to go up and down when you press on the pedal. I have gotten wonderful results from my old Bernina, which was built in the 1960s.

Learn how to care for your machine. If you are good to it, you will become partners in the work. Asking a machine to perform at high speeds for long periods of time can

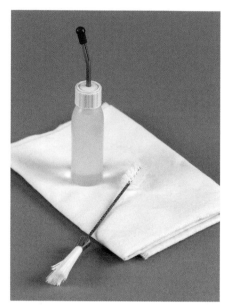

be hard on it. Brush away any lint every time you change the bobbin. Oil the upper machine and bobbin area as recommended in your machine's owner's manual. Each machine used may have varying requirements; be sure to read the book before beginning. Establishing a relationship with a dealer of the machine also can be valuable.

The maintenance of the exterior of your machine is another concern. Keep it clean and free from any sticky residue left from anything that has been attached to it.

Sewing Machine Feet

For free-motion quilting, use a darning or open-toe sewing machine foot, choosing whichever one gives you the best view of the needle. These feet can be used for curvilinear designs as well as straight lines and grids. If your machine is an older model, ask the dealer if there are newer options for free-motion quilting other than the feet that came with your machine. Keep in mind that this is refined work. A small foot gives a better view of the work and allows you to focus on a small area to fill with stitching.

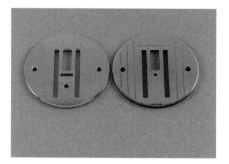

Single-Hole Throat Plate

You may benefit from using a single-hole throat plate for your machine. It has a small, circular opening for the needle to enter, rather than a wide hole that is needed for a zigzag stitch. The smaller hole keeps the quilting surface as flat as possible and prevents the fabric from being pushed down into the larger opening.

✂ tip

The stitch length setting on a sewing machine does not apply when the feed dogs are not being used to advance the fabric. The length of the stitches is entirely dependent upon how fast you move the fabric, compared with the speed the machine is stitching, which is controlled by the pressure of your foot on the pedal.

Machine Tension

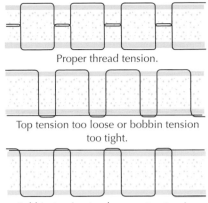

Proper thread tension.

Top tension too loose or bobbin tension too tight.

Bobbin tension too loose or top tension too tight.

Proper machine tension is imperative for achieving success in these projects. The stitches should catch each other in the middle of the quilt layers, and bobbin thread should not be seen on the top.

Always test the threads and needles to get the correct tension before stitching on the quilt. Make a quilt sandwich from the exact fabrics and batting used for each project as a practice sample.

Some machines will require adjustments to the tension when using lightweight threads; others will not. Learn to adjust the upper tension as well as the bobbin screw of the machine to accommodate thinner threads, if necessary. Consult the owner's manual for your machine to find the correct procedure to follow.

tip

Use this mnemonic device to remember how to tighten and loosen the bobbin screw: Righty tighty, lefty loosie.

The tension screw on the bobbin case may need to be tightened slightly if the adjustment of the machine's top tension alone does not result in proper stitches. Be sure to make very minor adjustments and do some test stitches to see if it looks correct before adjusting it again.

Note the original position of the bobbin screw before moving it. Reset it to that position when you are finished. A slight twist of the screw to the right will increase the grip on the thread.

Needles

The needle size must be coordinated to work with the size and style of the thread. Use only the recommended needles for your machine, and change them after eight hours of use. Continuous rapid use of the incorrect needle may damage the machine. Old, dull needles can cause skipped stitches and pulled threads, which in turn cause frustration.

Start fresh with a new needle in the machine, and try different styles of needles if you experience problems. Use a smaller needle with lightweight thread because it will produce smaller stitches and leave only tiny holes in the fabric.

A No. 70 sharp leaves a smaller hole than a No. 70 universal. For size 50 or 60 weight thread, use a size 70 or 80 needle. For 100-weight thread, use a size 60, 70 or 75 needle.

Thread

Machine quilting uses a lot of thread. Be sure you have a sufficient supply on hand before beginning a project. Purchase the best thread that you can afford. High-quality thread is worth every penny, and it eliminates problems that the cheap brands can create, such as lint and breakage.

Thread labels can be confusing. The higher the number, the finer the thread is. A 100-weight thread is very lightweight. Many designs used for heirloom machine quilting require the same line to be stitched more than once. A line of stitching can be retraced without an unsightly thread buildup when fine or invisible thread is used.

YLI offers 100-weight silk thread that can be used in the top and in the bobbin of a machine. This thread works well for very tiny stitching, and it transforms dull cotton fabric with a luxurious effect. It has a sheen that is perfect with elegant sateen fabric. YLI also makes 70- or 100-weight heirloom cotton thread. It is less expensive than the silk thread, and it can be used for both the top thread and in the bobbin. It has a more traditional look when used on cotton fabric. When silk is used for the top thread, you can save cost by using the 70-weight cotton in the bobbin.

Superior Threads offers The Bottom Line, a two-ply, 60-weight, lint-free polyester thread. It was designed for use in the bobbin when the top surface of a quilt was to be embellished with heavy thread decoration. It is ideal for many purposes when lightweight thread is recommended. I use it in both the top of the machine and the bobbin for heirloom machine quilting. It is available on large spools in a wide variety of colors, and it is reasonably priced, which makes this an attractive choice. If you are concerned about polyester thread because it may be stronger than the cotton fabric, consider that the projects in this book are all for home décor use, and they probably won't need to hold up against much wear. Also, these items are heavily quilted; any stress on one area of stitches is offset by other stitches within close proximity.

Other companies also make relatively lightweight threads for durable meandering on cotton fabric. They can be used for the top of the machine or in the bobbin.

Experiment with different brands and weights of threads to get the look you desire. When using lightweight or invisible threads, a thread stand may be necessary to achieve the proper tension.

Lightweight threads create special requirements of the operation of your machine. They may cause problems you never may have experienced when working with heavier threads. If the thread is fraying and breaking, there may be a snag somewhere along the thread path. Skipped stitches could indicate a timing problem with the machine. Contact a dealer for help with these situations.

Invisible thread, made of polyester or nylon, is used in the top of the machine only. It is available in clear for quilting light-colored fabrics and in smoke for more colorful fabrics. Invisible thread can get old and turn brittle. If it is breaking, buy new thread from a source that reorders its supply often.

Bobbin Thread

Use a lightweight thread in the bobbin to match the top thread or the backing fabric. Several different colors may be used in the same quilt if needed or desired. Use only bobbins made specifically for the machine by the machine's manufacturer, and make sure that they fill evenly. Save time during a large project by filling several extra bobbins.

Batting

Hobbs Heirloom Wool Batting was used for all of the projects in this book. It is wonderfully full bodied, it compresses nicely during the quilting process, but it springs back to fill all the shapes of the designs. The 100 percent wool batting is completely washable and is resin bonded to resist bearding. This batting is lightweight, which makes it a delight when maneuvering a large quilt. With it, trapunto was not needed to make the motifs stand out.

Battings made of 100 percent cotton or a blend of 80 percent cotton/20 percent polyester also are fine for these projects. The cotton in the batting shrinks, so preshrinking may be necessary unless an antique "puckered" look is desired. Be sure to check the batting package label for the amount of shrinkage to expect. These battings do not have the loft that the Hobbs wool does,

✄ tips

• Select thread that is a shade darker than your fabric. It will appear lighter when it is sewn into fabric and blend with the fabric color, which helps to hide slight variances in stitching off the design line.

• Lightweight thread goes a long way when filling a bobbin. Don't fill the bobbin too full if you only have one spool of thread.

• Try this to create extra tension for your machine's thread. Simply tape a safety pin on the right top corner of the back of your machine. Place the thread in a jar placed on the floor or next to the machine. Work the thread through the circular hole in the pin, then follow the machine's normal thread path.

which means the designs may need to be accentuated with trapunto. For more about machine trapunto, see Basic Techniques.

Polyester batting shifts and slides, which makes it an unfavorable choice for these projects.

Incidental Supplies

I recommend these supplies because they have worked well for me. Feel free to use these or similar items you already may have on hand. Be ready for any task or technique by keeping these supplies at hand when you are working on the projects in this book.

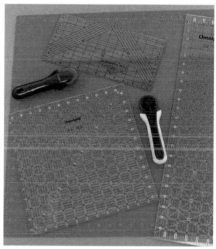

- **Plastic rulers, rotary cutter and mats.** It is unnecessary to have any specific ruler for these projects, although several were used in the construction process. These are essential tools for achieving accuracy in cutting pieces and strips and for squaring up the quilted projects.

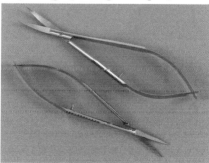

- **ez snips.** I really love this nice little tool from Specialty Scissors Sales

for trimming off the secured thread ends. The fine, serrated blades of the ez snips spring scissors, which originally were designed for eye surgery, safely cut the thread closer to the surface of the quilt than conventional scissors.

- **Free-Motion Slider.** A new, reusable Teflon® sheet, called the Free-Motion Slider, is designed to cover the bed of your machine. It makes the drag disappear and helps the quilt glide easily during any machine quilting. The result is a more consistent, free-motion stitch.

- **Pins.** Tiny gold pins in sizes 003 and 004 are good choices for basting these projects. They are lightweight and are made of a thin wire that leaves only small holes in the fabric. Straight pins also can be used to temporarily hold the layers of small projects together.

- **Heat-resistant fabric and batting for hot pads and table mats.** The Warm™ Company offers Insul-Bright®, a polyester insulating batting-like material that resists radiant heat. Other companies manufacture heat-resistant silver fabric that protects surfaces from heat.

- **Spray fabric protector.** Use spray fabric protector to treat household items and prevent spills from becoming stains on the projects. Always test a scrap of each fabric used in the project to ensure the spray does not adversely affect the fabric. Follow manufacturers' directions, and work in a well-ventilated space.

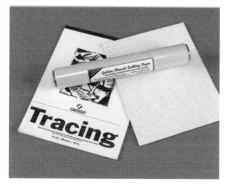

- **Tracing paper.** Use good-quality tracing paper available at art supply stores, or choose Quilting Paper by Golden Threads if you use the optional marking method detailed in Basic Techniques.

- **Water-soluble fabric marker.** Easily remove markings for patterns by using a water-soluble fabric marker. Simply submerge the finished project in cold water, and the markings will disappear. For more information on marking fabrics, see Basic Techniques.

- **Light box.** Whether you buy a light box or make your own following the tips in Basic Techniques, this tool is handy to have when transferring designs to fabric.

- **Glues.** A glue stick can be used to temporarily baste fabric. For permanent, quick-drying adhesion needed for the framing procedure, use the "thick as marshmallow cream" white glue typically sold in a jar.

- **Tapes.** Acid-free mounting tape, which is used for the framing process, is available in ¾" and 1" widths. It can be found at scrapbooking or framing stores. Masking tape is used to hold patterns and fabrics to the light box and to hold the quilt layers for pin basting.

- **Acid-free mat board**. Use this to mount framed artwork. It is available at frame shops or craft supply stores.

- **A chopstick or blunt wooden dowel.** These tools are valuable when turning pillows, leaves and napkin rings right side out and persuading points to come out crisp.

- **Fusible web.** I used fusible web that is sold in rolls that measure ½" wide. Where larger pieces are needed, such as the Autumn Leaves Coasters, I use paper-backed fusible web.

- **Other miscellaneous supplies**: Iron, ironing board and scissors.

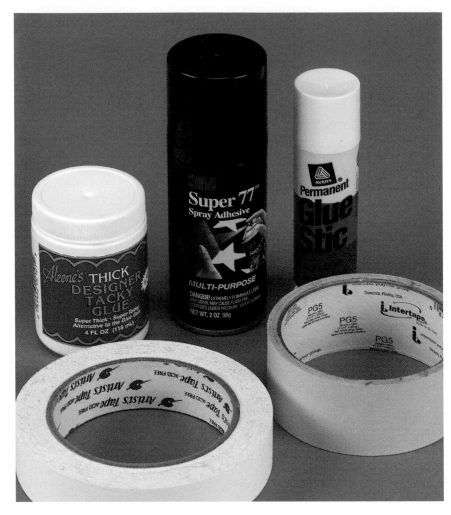

Fabric Choices and Conditioning

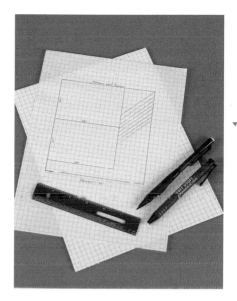

Calculating Yardage

The fabric requirements given for each project reflect the amount of fabric you need to purchase when making only that item. The supply list will indicate if the fabric used for the top also is used for the backing. Make adjustments to this amount if a different fabric is chosen for the backing.

It also is a good idea to draw a cutting plan on graph paper if you haven't had a lot of experience with sewing. Draw the project's top and backing, and allow extra space when cutting bias strips for matching binding.

Project cutting instructions include a little extra fabric to give you something to hold onto during the quilting process. That extra fabric is trimmed away later in the project.

If you make more than one project from the same fabric, the total amount of fabric required may be less than the amount needed to make both pieces individually. Use a piece of graph paper to draw the cutting sizes of all of the required pieces to get an accurate assessment of your needs.

Choosing Fabrics

Use 100 percent cotton fabric of the best quality that you can afford. Using a light-colored solid fabric will make it easier to trace the pattern lines. RJR makes cotton sateen in solid colors with a sheen that will highlight the elegant quilting designs. For projects that use prints, choose a theme print fabric first; then base the solid color choices on the print.

Don't cut corners on the backing fabric. Avoid poorly woven, inexpensive fabrics for the back of your work, because that can cause headaches you don't need. They can stretch, or if they are printed with stiff paint, they can drag on the bed of the machine during the quilting process. A good-quality print that blends nicely with your project will hide any inexperienced stitching.

Washing, Storing and Stabilizing Fabric

Prewashing is recommended for all fabrics. Prewashing will preshrink fabric and test it for colorfastness. After the quilting has been completed, the items will need to

tips

• If you choose sateen for these projects, remember that the fabric has a lustrous sheen, and it needs to be cut and assembled with all of the pieces running in the same direction. When cutting sateen, use a pin or sticker to indicate the top of each piece and to help keep the fabric organized.

• One of the keys to success in machine quilting is having a project with a flat, accurately pieced top that is free of bumps that could interrupt your stitching rhythm. Press seams open to equalize the thickness of the fabric layers.

be submerged in cold water to remove the marking lines; prewashing the fabrics should prevent further shrinkage or distortion from fabrics that shrink in differing amounts.

Wash each fabric in a white sink to see whether the color bleeds. If bleeding persists, either soak the fabric in a product that will set the color permanently or choose another fabric.

After the fabric is washed, partially dry it in the dryer. Press the damp fabric completely dry, and store it flat.

Spray starch will stabilize the fabric when it is cut and stitched. It also will help keep the markings from a water-soluble marker from penetrating the fabric, making the lines easier to remove. To avoid flaking, spray the fabric and let the starch penetrate for a few minutes. Don't worry if a drop of spray starch shows up on a solid fabric as a spot; it will wash out when the finished piece is submerged in cold water to remove the markings.

Keeping Records

Sometimes the world interrupts our quilting schedules, and our memories become overloaded. That's when a quilting journal comes in handy.

Use a notebook, scrapbook or pocket file to hold information regarding each project you begin. Keep it handy as you work so you quickly can record any additions. Quilting journal information can include:

• The amount of fabric purchased, as well as where and when each piece was bought.

• A time log for how long processes took.

• Thread colors, manufacturers and the number of spools purchased. Heirloom machine quilting uses a lot of thread, so keeping track can be especially beneficial when figuring future needs. If you run out, you will be thankful you have the color number recorded.

• The needle's size and number of hours used. Be sure to change each needle after eight hours of use to ensure the best results.

• Any adjustments to the bobbin case. Indicate where it was when you started, so you can return it to the original position for normal sewing.

• Appliqué settings, stitch length and stitch width. If you get interrupted, you can return to the exact same settings to duplicate the look.

• Important events that are happening in the world.

• Why you are making this piece and your feelings for the person for whom you are making it.

Besides being a practical source of project information, a quilting journal will bring you joy when you read it after the project is finished, and for years to come.

Sewing Space Setup

Choose Proper Furniture and Lighting

Set up your sewing area properly to avoid aches and pains. Use a large table with a smooth surface to support the entire project. A table height of about 30" should allow your elbows to bend at a 90-degree angle. Use an adjustable-height office chair that has good back support. Sit with your body directly aligned with the needle. Sitting off center may cause stress on your back, and it also distorts your view of the work.

Proper lighting is vital when following intricate pattern lines. Try directing the lighting from different angles to determine which setup works best for you. Switch off the machine light to see if that may help you see the pattern lines better.

Avoid Fatigue

Stop stitching every half hour, and stand up and walk around. Stretch your body, and rotate your wrists and ankles; the stretching will relax you.

Look out the window to give your eyes a break. Be sure your eyeglass prescription is accurate for detail work. You also may find a magnifying glass to be beneficial when sewing.

There are many quilter's aids now available to move fabric around when machine quilting. Whatever method you use, try to eliminate any stress on your body. If you are wearing gloves, make sure that they are not too tight or cutting off the circulation to your hands. Quilting rings and mice require you to grip them tightly and bend your wrists, causing tension on your body. Try just spreading out your fingers and pushing the fabric, allowing your wrists to stay straight.

tips

• Use eye drops when you sew for prolonged periods of time. The drops will soothe your eyes.

• Are you hunting for tools and tips to make quilting more comfortable? Check out the Web site http://www.painfreequilting.com for ideas to take the pain and strain out of your work.

Wondering where to start and what to do? Check in this chapter to learn how to prepare the top for quilting, how to trace the patterns from the large pattern pullout sheet, how to alter pattern sizes and how to stitch designs. Information on marking the designs on the fabric will help you make the right choices for these projects, and tips on basting will help you get ready to put the needle in the fabric. I also give you the terminology used for this craft so you can sound like a pro!

Basic Techniques

Elements of Heirloom Machine Quilting

Heirloom machine quilting is accomplished using refined free-motion techniques. The feed dogs of the sewing machine are lowered, and a darning foot is attached. The operator controls the stitch length and direction of the stitching line by moving the quilt with her hands. Pattern lines are drawn on the quilt top and are followed to produce decorative motifs.

Just as with the tool suggestions in Getting Started, some methods I suggest may differ from what you were taught or have done in the past. The instructions included in the book have worked for me. However, if you feel you know a better way to proceed, do whatever works for you to get the best results.

Background Quilting

Quilts that have been heirloom machine quilted usually include background quilting, which fills the negative space around the designs with dense stitching. This creates contrast between the curvilinear shapes and the flattened background space. This can be achieved using stippling, echo quilting, repeated patterns or geometric grids.

Stippling and Meandering

When you look at the heirloom machine quilted artwork in this book, you see the impressive impact of stippling, the tiny puzzle-piece shaped lines surrounding the motifs. Stippling uses the same process of stitching a continuous curved line as is used for the larger version, which is

called meandering. In stippling, however, the scale is reduced. When lines of stitching are less than ¼" apart, they are referred to as stippling.

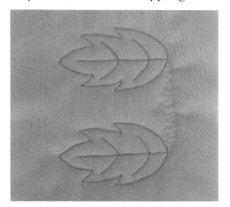

Meandering or stippling lines are not drawn onto the quilt; they are stitched after the motifs are completed. Stippling also can be used as a vehicle to travel from one large element of the design to another without cutting the thread.

Visualize the blank space to be filled with stippling before you begin. Start at the bottom of that area and work away from yourself. This will give you the best view of where you have been and where you need to go next.

Echo Quilting

With echo quilting, the outer shape of a motif is followed with rows of stitching lines that are an equal distance from each another.

✂ tip

Remember to lower the presser foot when you are free-motion quilting.

When numerous rows are used, they give the effect of tiny ripples on the surface of a lake. Use just a row or two, or stitch as many rows as it takes to fill the background space until you meet another shape.

Straight-Line Grids

Straight-line grids fill in large, empty spaces of projects, creating a strong contrast to curved shapes. Grids traditionally have been used in the home decorating field and fashion industry as an effective way to accentuate elegant curving designs. Grid lines can be drawn parallel to the edges of the quilt or on the diagonal, with varying degrees of the angle. Straight-line grids can be free-motion quilted or stitched with the aid of a walking foot. Focus on the line to be stitched, not on the needle.

When planning a grid, pay close attention to where grid lines meet or cross the design, and make adjustments to gain pleasing results. Make sure the grid line is drawn from edge to edge of the design area, centering the curvilinear design over the grid. Work out the intersection of

the grid and the parameters of the space to be filled on paper before you mark your quilt.

Any background quilting pattern that you decide to use should touch the edge of the design it is next to and fill the space up to the binding of the quilt. All types of quilting need to be evenly distributed throughout your entire quilt. Uneven amounts of quilting distort the quilt and cause wavy edges. Areas that are left without quilting look unfinished.

Foundation Anchoring

Many quilters rely on walking foot attachments for their sewing machines to stitch foundations around patchwork blocks and along borders to anchor the layers together, and they use free-motion quilting

for stitching the curvilinear motifs. The stitches made with the walking foot will look different from those of hand-guided work. This may be objectionable or of little consequence to your piece. Accomplished heirloom machine quilters use free-motion techniques for the entire quilting process.

If you are using a walking foot for part of the process, shorten your stitch length to match the look of your free-motion stitch length, which usually is quite small.

✂ Just for grins

In my class with Diane Gaudynski, she suggested that students make Mickey Mouse ears and little mitten shapes for stippling. I was in Houston instructing my aunt on how to stipple when I used Diane's examples.

When I looked at her work I said, "What are you doing?"

She said, "Just a minute. Three, four, five, there!"

I guess there have been just too many years since she left her beloved Wisconsin winters, because she was stitching gloves with all five fingers.

Trapunto

Trapunto refers to a technique used to accentuate specific motifs of a quilting design by adding an extra layer of batting. Heirloom machine quilters have invented a new, faster machine method known as heirloom machine trapunto. It is an extra step that is done before the usual layers are assembled for quilting.

For heirloom machine trapunto, transfer the entire quilting design to the quilt top with water erasable marker, just as you would for regular quilting. Then place a layer of wool or polyester batting under the marked top, and pin-baste only these two layers together. Use water-soluble thread in the top of the machine and lightweight thread in the bobbin to stitch a line around each motif that is to be accentuated.

Next, remove the basting pins and cut away the excess batting from all areas that are not to be padded. When that is complete, the regu-

lar batting and backing are added. Basting and quilting continues in the regular manner using the usual thread, as if no trapunto is used.

After the quilting and stippling are completed, the quilt is submerged in cold water to remove the

markings and the thread used for the trapunto. Be sure to evenly distribute the trapunto throughout the quilt, and do not add more than one layer of batting for the trapunto. Too much extra padding may distort the shape of the quilt.

tip

I mention trapunto for your information, even though it is not used for the projects in this book. Since I have been using Hobbs Heirloom Wool batting, I have found it unnecessary to add any further padding to highlight the designs. I offer you this instruction in case you

choose to use another batting that needs to have fullness added to make the motifs stand out.

Altering Patterns

The size of the quilting designs used for the projects in this book can be altered for use in other quilting projects. Use a copy machine and this guide for common sizes, or use a proportion wheel to adjust them to any size you need. Here are guidelines to increase or decrease a design that originally is 8" x 8":

• **For a 6" x 6" square:** Set the copier at 75 percent.
• **For a 10" x 10" square:** Set the copier at 125 percent.
• **For a 12" x 12" square:** Set the copier at 150 percent.

Inverting Designs

To invert the direction of a design and yield a mirror image of the original, follow these steps.

1. Carefully trace the lines on tracing paper.

2. Flip the paper over.

3. Trace the lines from the back, or photocopy the design with a white sheet of paper on top of the tracing paper.

Adjusting Grids

You may wish to adjust the sizes of these projects to fit your specific requirements. But adjusting designs that include a grid can be a little tricky.

• **To enlarge the entire pattern:** Set the copy machine to reproduce the image at the percentage of increase needed. Make as many copies as needed to complete the design.

• **To alter the length of the grid:** Slide the pattern forward or backward in complete diamond increments. Match the row of diamonds across the entire width of the design. Trace as many rows as need to be added.

Marking Basics

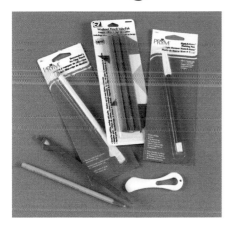

Choosing a Marking Tool

Many marking tools are available. Whatever tool you choose, use a light touch. The less you put on, the less you have to take off.

Water-soluble markers are available in blue for light colors or white pencils for dark fabrics. Before using markers, test them on all fabrics on which they will be used. Never iron any fabric that has been marked; this could set the markings in the fabric permanently.

Removing Markings

To remove markings, submerge the entire piece in cold water until the lines are completely gone.

Remove the piece from the water, and lay it flat to dry. Never wring the quilted piece; rather, blot it with absorbent towels to remove some excess water.

The quilt may need some blocking. Lay it flat on a water resistant surface. Gently persuade it into shape with your hands: Let it know who is boss. Place a fan near it for faster drying.

Using Light Boxes

A light box may be necessary when transferring the designs to dark fabrics. Tape the paper design to the lighted surface. Carefully center the fabric over the paper design and tape it down to avoid slipping.

There are many commercially made light boxes available, but you can try some items that may already be around the house to get the same effect.

A day-lit window on a sunny side of your house can provide enough light for tracing. Or, you can place an under-counter strip light inside an inverted flat-bottomed plastic storage box.

For large projects, use a table that slides apart to accommodate an extension leaf. Slide the sides of the table apart as you would if you were putting the table leaf in place. Cover the tabletop to protect it. Position a clean window from a storm door over the gap where the leaf would go and place a lamp on the floor under the table to create large, lighted work surface.

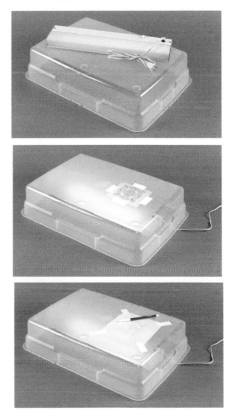

Paper removal tips: Gently tug the quilted piece on the diagonal to pop the paper away from the stitching. For straight lines, fold and gently tear away paper as if you are removing a check from a checkbook. Be sure that you remove all of the paper. This can be a tedious procedure, but you can try using a pin to pick tiny paper fibers out from under stitches. Use a loop of masking tape to pick up any tiny bits of paper that remain.

Basting

When the quilt top has been assembled and the backing fabric has been conditioned using the procedures indicated in Getting Started, it is time to baste the layers for quilting.

Get started by choosing a hard work surface that is at a comfortable height for you to stand and work, such as a kitchen counter.

Machine quilters baste the layers of their quilts with safety pins rather than thread, because thread would get caught in the stitches during the quilting process. I use tiny, gold safety pins in sizes 0003 and 0004. The pins are inexpensive, and they do not get in the way while I am quilting. The thin, soft metal leaves a smaller hole in the fabric and makes the pins very easy to open and close.

Trace and Stitch Marking Method

A few designs in this book are quite small, have intricate components and are a bit more challenging to mark and stitch. You can work around this by tracing the design on tracing paper, then stitching through the paper. This marking method may be great for dark fabric, but with light-colored fabric, ink could show up during laundering if left behind on paper fragments.

Practice this marking method on a sample piece of fabric and wash it before you use it on the final project piece. Here are the steps:

1. Copy the design onto tracing paper or quilting paper with a fine-line permanent marker. Do not use pencil.
2. Accurately position the design on the fabric. Pin it securely in place.
3. Stitch the design right through the paper. Only the motifs are stitched with the paper attached.
4. Remove all of the paper fragments before any background quilting is done. Avoid pulling on the stitches.

Pin Basting

1. Securely tape the backing fabric to the counter, wrong side up, with masking tape. Avoid stretching the layers when basting, because this will cause puckering during the quilting process.
2. Smooth the batting on top of the backing.
3. Center the top over the first two layers. Use tape to hold it down securely.
4. Start from the center and working outward, pinning every 4" or 5". Avoid the pattern lines whenever possible.

5. Place a pin along the edges at 4" intervals.

6. When finished, gently remove the tape from all of the layers, using caution so that the fabric edge does not ravel.

Straight pin option: Straight pins may be adequate to hold the layers of some tiny projects together during quilting. Slide a pin into the layers, making sure to end with the point on the top surface of the quilt sandwich so the pin won't catch on anything.

Traveling Guide

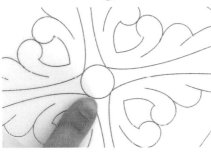

Practice First

Before you begin working on the real project, it's important to know the best place to start each design and how to direct your line of stitching. Understanding how to complete the pattern before you try to stitch it onto the fabric will allow you to concentrate on simply following the line. Use these tips to help alleviate stress.

Learn the Design

Trace the design on the paper pattern with your finger. Begin at the point indicated with the start arrow. Travel around the entire design to familiarize yourself with the direction of travel and the shapes that need to be made to complete the motif. Discover where it may be necessary to stop and start a new thread before you are stitching in the fabric.

Now try it again, observing the repetitive segments of designs, such as scallops and leaves. Make up a stitching rhythm by counting the time it takes to complete one section of the design. For instance, it takes three counts to go up one side of the leaf and three counts to come down the other side. This exercise strengthens the connection between tracing with your finger and tracing the line with thread. First visualize the shape, and then add a rhythm. Your stitch length will be more consistent.

When you are ready to stitch, unthread the machine and guide the machine over the shapes of the design marked on the fabric. Just try to stay on the lines, over and over again, until you are comfortable with the movement.

Practice like this until you are moving the quilt sandwich around under the needle with ease. With any luck you will avoid getting hung up on stitch length before you feel comfortable with the movement of your hands tracing the design with the machine.

Starting and Stopping Your Stitching

Once you have imprinted a pattern in your brain, attached the darning foot to your sewing machine, lowered the feed dogs and presser foot and tested the thread tension, it's time to stitch.

An important element in the overall success of your project is how and where to start a line of stitching. Begin in an area of the design that will be hidden by more stitching that will cross it later. Insert the needle and rotate the flywheel one entire turn, stopping with the needle at its highest point. This will bring the bobbin thread up so you can pull it through to the top.

Return the needle to the fabric. Hold both threads out of the way, and take four or five stitches very close together. This will hold the thread securely. Stitching in exactly the same place will cause an unsightly buildup of thread.

Begin stitching by following the marked line. Stop stitching with the needle down in the fabric about 2" away from where you began. Clip your threads off at the surface of the quilt.

Coordinate the speed of the machine with the movement of your hands. Focus on the direction in which you are moving and the line to be stitched, not on the needle. Vary your speed with the intricacy of the design. Any time you are unsure where to proceed, take your foot off the pedal and stop with needle down.

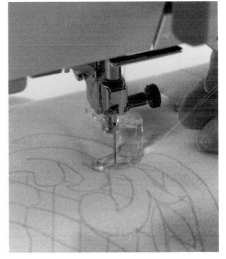

To finish a line of stitching, take four or five stitches very close together, then snip off the threads. If you run out of bobbin thread unexpectedly, clip the top thread and begin the new line of stitching ¼" back, right on top of the stitched line you were sewing before you ran out.

Following Quilting Sequences

Each pattern in this book has a specific sequence to follow for each design. This is a wonderful tool to help you make the least number of starts and stops and understand how to travel from one area of the design to the next. These guides are helpful for these projects and will help you understand how to navigate the design in your future projects.

Basic Quilting Sequence

1. Stabilize the layers by stitching the long, straight lines of the design, or by stitching along borders first.
2. Next, follow the outlines of the motifs.

3. Fill in the details of the motifs.
4. Once large designs are finished, fill in background grids and stippling.

When you quilt from one area of the design to another, stop with the needle down in the fabric. Determine if you can proceed to the next area without having to cut the thread. There are times you may travel, or "drive," to the place you need to go next by retracing a short distance on a previously quilted line. You also may move along the outer edge of the project where the stitching will be hidden in the binding. Or, there are situations when you may travel to the next motif with a worm-like line of stippling, if that is the chosen background filler.

When filling large areas with stippling, begin at one edge and work away from yourself. Fill in a 1" wide strip all the way across the area. Vary the width and pattern of this stitching so that successive bands are hidden and intermingle with one another.

Stippling or background quilting should touch the edges of the motifs it borders. Fill the space up to the binding of the quilt. Inconsistency is a good thing in the stippling pattern. Try to avoid repeating the exact shape over and over—and the "rivers" that may form when the lines aren't blended well. Keep your lines an equal distance from one another.

Here's an easy way to get in and back out of small spaces when you encounter narrow spaces between motifs, such as in the leaf border on the Autumn Leaves Heat-Resistant Trivet design on pages 34-37. Stitch little humps all along one side of the narrow passage, then retrace the outline of the shape along the other edge to get back out; otherwise the stitching looks too full or like a zigzag between the designs.

Stitching Grids

For most of the quilting sequences in this book that use a grid, the outline of the space to be filled in is stitched before you start the grid. Try these tips for great grids:

For a grid that is inside a square or rectangular outline:

1. Stitch the entire outline of the rectangle. Stop with the needle down at the intersection of the nearest grid line.
2. Follow that line of the grid to the other end of the line. Stop with the needle down in the fabric.
3. Pivot 90 degrees at the point where the line meets the outline; rotate the fabric if it feels more comfortable.
4. Proceed across the design in the other direction until you meet the outside edge of the design.
5. Continue until the grid is complete. There may be times that it will be necessary to retrace your line of stitching along the outline to get to the next line of the grid. End with the needle down, then decide if you can travel to the next area to be stitched or if you need to end the line of stitching and snip the thread.

For a grid inside of a square or rectangular outline that has a design in the corners and/or center:

Follow the same procedures used for square or rectangular outlines, except when the line of stitching runs into the outline of the design. In that case, retrace the outline of the design to get to the next grid line.

For the heart filled with the diamond grid:

The lines end at the outline of the heart. Follow the outline to the next grid line that needs to be stitched.

Removing Unwanted Stitches

To rip or not to rip? That is the question.

It is so disappointing when you stitch off the line. Tearing out these tiny stitches can be done, but it is a tedious job. I work from the back, finding a place where I can slide my seam ripper in to cut the thread. Then I coax it under the next stitch, and soon I have a snippet of bobbin thread long enough that I can grab onto. I then pull on that thread and pull the top thread to the back, and tug and slip until the mistake is gone.

Planning and Practice

Who among us cannot spare a square for a practice sample?

Before you begin a project from the book, transfer the design to a solid fabric, set up a practice "sandwich" of fabric and batting, and give it a try. Consider that you are investing a minimal amount of fabric and time compared with the potential gain of perfecting this skill and completing the beautiful projects.

The projects in this book are relatively small and easy to maneuver under the needle. Have a positive outlook, and try to relax while you are stitching. Mental tension causes fatigue.

In trying any new experience in life, discomfort is a source of motivation. When your brain is outside its comfort zone, it will prompt you to change, try new procedures, and, I hope, work until you get it right.

✕ tips

• Use a plastic ruler as a guide when stitching straight rows. Place the needle down into the fabric, lower the darning foot, and lay the ruler next to the foot and exactly parallel to the drawn lines of the pattern. Hold the ruler against the fabric and let the foot glide along the straight edge.

• Keep mistakes in perspective. If the mistake can be covered with stippling and the line possibly reshaped, and if it is off by just a bit, no one else will ever know after the marked lines are rinsed away. Or just say, "That one camel is supposed to look like a fire hydrant!"

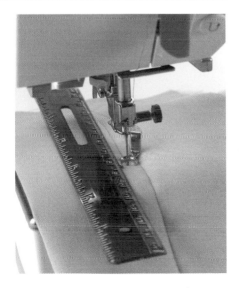

Impress your guests with your quilting skills and this beautiful yet easily constructed collection of dining accessories. A variety of quilting designs that surround an autumnal theme create this grouping.

Choose a large-scale fall print and several rich sateen fabrics that accentuate the quilted leaf designs. The print should have large leaves that can be cut out and used individually as appliqués or decorative accents. Follow the easy instructions to construct this lovely table display complete with all the accessories needed to serve a grand feast.

Autumn Leaves

Autumn Leaves Table Runner

Autumn Leaves Table Runner, 16" x 26".

Simple abundance describes the elegant combination of glowing sateen with the formal simplicity of the quilted leaf border of the Autumn Leaves Table Runner. You can create it as the cornerstone for your autumnal dining room décor. The glow from the sateen fabric accentuates the softly curving leaf pattern against the contrasting geometric grid.

While the border may look like each leaf must be stitched separately, the pattern is simply two lines of stitching that travel all the way around the rectangle. This runner is so pretty and so quick to make, you may want to make one for your dining table and another for your buffet.

materials

fabric

- 1¼ yd. sateen or solid-colored fabric for top, backing and binding

notions

- Fall Leaves Table Runner pattern from pullout
- 20" x 30" piece of batting
- Lightweight thread to match the fabric

Cut

1. Cut two 20" x 30" pieces from the sateen or solid-colored fabric, one each for the top and backing. This is 2" larger than the finished design on all sides, but the extra fabric provides something to hold onto during the quilting process.

2. Cut one 20" x 30" piece of batting.

3. Cut enough 2¼" wide bias strips from the sateen or solid-colored fabric to make 94" of double-fold binding.

Mark

1. Make two copies of the Autumn Leaves Table Runner design from the pattern pullout. Match the dotted lines that indicate the center of the design. Tape the two halves together to make an entire design.

2. Tape the completed pattern to a hard surface or light box, if it is necessary to see the pattern lines through the fabric.

3. Fold your top fabric in half in both directions, and gently crease it. Use this line to center the fabric over the paper pattern, matching the fold lines in the fabric to the dotted lines on the pattern and tape it in place.

4. Using a water-soluble pen, carefully trace the design onto the fabric. Take your time, and use a long ruler as a guide for all of the straight lines.

Quilt

1. Assemble the layers for quilting. See Basic Techniques for details.

2. Pin baste the layers in place. Avoid placing pins on the stitching lines.

3. Study the quilting sequence and complete a practice sample. See Basic Techniques for details.

4. Stitch around the outer rectange outline to anchor the layers. Secure the thread.

5. Start quilting the center rectangle; begin near a corner. Complete the outer line of the design, and end just beyond the starting point. Secure the thread.

6. Stitch around the inner row. Stop with the needle in the fabric just past the starting point.

7. Travel to the nearest grid line. Begin to fill in the grid.

8. Stitch the grid with one continuous line. Pivot at each intersection of the rectangle, and continue in the other direction. There may be occasions when it will be necessary to retrace the stitching line of the rectangle to get to the next grid line. Refer to Basic Techniques for more information about stitching a grid.

9. Stitch the leaf outline that is closest to the center of the quilt. While it may look like each leaf must be stitched separately, there

✂ tips

• Consider using some special products with the Autumn Leaves projects. For instance, manufactured spray fabric protector can be used to prevent stains from food spills, while other products can protect your table. Insul-Bright, a batting-like material, helps resist radiant heat, and heat-proof silver fabric can be used as a backing material.

• Before you begin a project, take time to practice each pattern on your practice sample. Refer to Basic Techniques for information on beginning and ending the threads.

are only two lines of stitching that travel all the way around the rectangle. Stitch all the way around the design, and stop just past the beginning point. Secure the thread.

10. Begin the second row of the leaf border by securing the thread at the base of any leaf vein.

11. Stitch the vein by moving outward, then return to the center with one line of stitching exactly on top of the first line of stitching. Stitch to the opposite side and back, and then stitch up the center to the second set of veins.

12. Continue to stitch each vein up to the top of the leaf. Return back down the centerline, going over the stitches that already are there.

13. Follow the curve from the center vein over to the leaf outline. Stitch up and around to complete the outline of the leaf.

14. Stitch past the starting point, and go on to the next leaf's center vein.

15. Complete the remaining border of leaves using one thread. Stitch the veins and outlines of each leaf, and connect it to the next one with the scalloped stem.

16. Fill the space between the center grid and the leaf border with stippling. Refer to Basic Techniques for tips on filling a large area.

Finish

1. Once you finish quilting, submerge the entire piece in cold water to remove markings. Lay the piece flat to dry.

2. Place the dry piece on a cutting mat. Trim it to measure 16" x 26".

3. Attach the bias binding. Refer to Finishing Touches for more information on bindings.

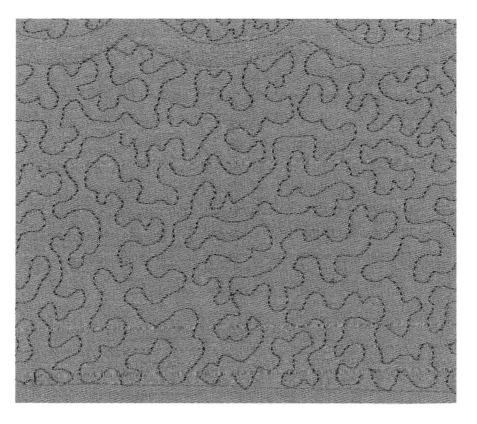

Autumn Leaves Heat-Resistant Trivet, 12" x 12".

Here is a pretty way to protect your table from damage by hot dishes. This practical little mat features two of the leaf motifs, which form a circular pattern. With just a few minutes and a few squares of fabric, you can make one for the table and another to keep near the oven. If you use heat-resistant batting, this quilted pad can be used to carry hot food.

materials

fabric

- ½ yd. sateen fabric for top and bias binding
- ½ yd. heat-resistant silver fabric for backing

notions

- Trivet pattern from pullout
- 16" x 16" piece of insulated batting
- Lightweight thread to match the top fabric

Cut

1. Cut one 16" x 16" piece from the sateen. This actually is 2" larger on all sides than the finished design will be, but the extra fabric will give you something to hold on to while you are quilting.

2. Cut one 16" x 16" piece from the backing fabric.

3. Cut one 16" x 16" piece from the batting.

4. Cut enough 2¼" wide strips from the sateen to make 58" of double-fold bias binding. Refer to Finishing Touches for binding instructions.

Mark

1. Copy the Trivet pattern from the pattern pullout in the back of the book. Tape it to a hard surface, or light box, if necessary.

2. Gently crease a fold in the center of the fabric; fold across the width and down the length of the square.

3. Center the fabric square over the paper design. Tape it in place. If necessary, use a light table to aid in tracing.

4. Carefully trace the leaf pattern lines onto the fabric with a water-soluble pen.

5. Using a ruler, trace the straight lines and a 12" square to indicate the final project outline.

Quilt

1. Assemble the layers for quilting as directed in Basic Techniques.

2. Study the quilting sequence, and complete a practice sample to familiarize yourself with the pattern. Refer to Basic Techniques for additional information.

3. Anchor the layers by stitching the double outlines that make up the center square. Stitch the outer line first, and then the inner line. Each line will use a separate thread.

4. Stitch the inner scalloped line of the circular leaf design first. Secure the thread.

5. Quilt the circular leaf design. Refer to the instructions for the Autumn Leaves Table Runner project to learn how the outline and veins of the oval leaves are stitched with one thread.

6. Complete the circular leaf pattern by stitching the inner scalloped line first. Secure the thread.

7. Stipple the background (optional). Fill the entire area with tiny stippling, touching the edges of the leaves and filling the space just beyond the outline of the square. Refer to Basic Techniques for tips on stippling.

8. Sew a final row around the outer edge of the square to hold the layers in place.

9. Quilt the entire piece. Refer to the basic quilting techniques in Basic Techniques.

tip

When making multiples of a project, you may need less fabric than you think. Rather than automatically multiplying the fabric yardage by the number of projects you plan to make, use a piece of graph paper to lay out the cutting sizes and assess what supplies are needed.

Finish

1. When quilting is complete, submerge the piece in cold water to remove markings. Lay it flat to dry.

2. Square up the piece by laying it on a cutting mat, and trimming it to a 12" square.

3. Attach the bias binding according to the instructions in Finishing Touches.

4. Spray the piece with a fabric protector to help prevent any stains.

Autumn Leaves Place Mat, 12" x 18".

Combine a warm-toned solid fabric with a large-scale fall print to make these pretty and practical place mats. Simple construction techniques make them a snap to complete!

Mix and match your solid fabric and prints to create a set with contrasting binding. The yardage given is for four place mats; adjust the materials list to fit your needs.

materials (for four place mats)
fabric

- ½ yd. fall print fabric for mat centers
- 1¼ yd. sateen or solid fabric for borders and binding
- 1¼ yd. fabric for backing (either same as top or contrasting fabric)

notions

- Place Mat pattern from pullout
- 45" x 60" batting
- Lightweight thread to match the solid fabric and quilt the leaf pattern
- Smoke-colored invisible thread to quilt the print fabric
- Lightweight thread for bobbin to match to the backing fabric

Cut

1. Cut one 8½" x 14½" piece from the fall print fabric.

2. Cut two 3¼" x 14¼" pieces from the solid fabric for the top and bottom strips. Keep the sheen of the fabric running in the same direction for the entire project.

3. Cut two 3¼" x 14½" pieces from the solid fabric for the side strips.

4. Cut one 14" x 20" piece from the backing fabric.

5. Cut one 14" x 20" piece from the batting.

6. Cut enough 2¼" wide bias strips from the solid fabric to make 70" of double-fold binding for each place mat. This project uses a lot of bias binding; keep that in mind when cutting out the pieces so you can cut those strips as long as possible. Make a layout on graph paper to make the best use of the fabric.

7. Repeat Steps 1 through 6 for the remaining place mats.

Assemble

1. Sew the top and bottom solid strips to the center panel. If you are using sateen, remember to keep the strips running in the same direction.

2. Press the seams open.

3. Sew on the side strips. Keep the strips running in the same direction if using sateen.

4. Press seams open.

5. Repeat Steps 1 through 4 for the remaining place mats.

Mark

1. Copy the Place Mat design from the pattern pullout sheet.

2. Tape the design to a hard surface or light box if it is necessary to see the pattern lines through the fabric.

3. Center the fabric over the paper pattern. The pattern is printed with a dotted line indicating the center of the design in each direction. There will be ¼" of space around the print fabric before the leaf design begins.

4. Using a water-soluble pen, carefully trace the design onto the fabric.

5. Draw an outline 2¼" away from the print fabric. This will be the cutting line when the quilting is complete.

6. Repeat Steps 1 through 5 for the remaining place mats.

Quilt

1. Assemble the layers for quilting and pin baste, as directed in Basic Techniques. Avoid placing pins on the stitching lines.

2. Study the quilting sequence. Note that halves of two leaves form circles around the entire outline. Complete a practice sample to familiarize yourself with the pattern and ensure your machine's settings are correct. Refer to Basic Techniques for additional information.

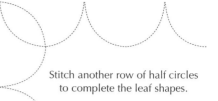

Stitch another row of half circles to complete the leaf shapes.

3. Using invisible smoke-colored thread in the top of the machine and a lightweight thread to match the backing fabric in the bobbin, anchor the layers in the seam line around the edge of the fall print. Follow the outlines and veins of the printed leaves as a guide for quilting the print fabric. Stitch as many details needed to evenly distribute the quilting.

4. Change the thread to a lightweight thread to match the solid fabric.

5. Begin quilting the leaf border by stitching the outlines of any two leaves that are next to each other to form a half circle. Stitch one row of half circles around the entire edge, returning to the starting point. At each corner, stitch around the entire leaf outline, and then stitch the half circles of the next side of the border.

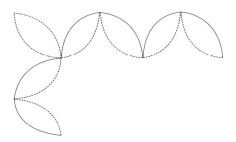

6. Stitch the inner row of half circles that will complete the leaf outlines. Skip the corner leaves on this pass. End with the thread in the fabric at the tip of a leaf.

7. Fill in the leaf veins. Start at the leaf tip. Move down the center to the intersection of the first vein. Stitch over to one side, then stitch back on the same line to the center and continue on to the opposite outer edge. From there, move up the outer edge to the next vein, and so on to the top of the leaf. There the vein from the first leaf will connect to the vein of the next leaf in the row. The same procedure is followed form leaf to leaf around the entire border.

✄ tip

When using sateen for a pieced project, cut the two side border strips perpendicular to the two end strips and mark them to keep the sheen running in the same direction.

8. If desired, stipple the background around the leaves. Remember to touch the edges of the leaves and fill the space beyond the outline of the finished piece.

9. Repeat Steps 1 through 8 for the remaining place mats.

Finish

1. When quilting is complete, submerge the entire piece in cold water to remove markings. Lay the piece flat to dry.

2. Lay the mat on a cutting mat. Trim the edges evenly on all sides to reach a finished size of 12" x 18".

3. Attach the bias binding. Refer to the directions in Finishing Touches.

4. If desired, spray the finished place mat with fabric protector.

5. Repeat Steps 1 through 4 for the remaining place mats.

Autumn Leaves Napkins

Autumn Leaves Napkin, 16" x 16", folded and paired with coordinating Autumn Leaves Napkin Ring featured on page 46.

Use this fast, no-sew technique to make a set of four print napkins to match the rest of the fall table ensemble.

The edges have been pressed under in a double hem and fused using strips of fusible web. While the hems can be permanently held with the fusible web, this is a great opportunity to use some of the decorative stitches available on your machine to dress up the napkins.

Check your owner's manual for directions on how to set up your sewing machine for some of those seldom-used stitches. You also may choose to use a serger to overcast the edges with a decorative thread.

materials (for four napkins)

fabric

- 1 yd. fall print fabric or contrasting solid fabric

notions

- ½" wide roll of fusible web
- Lightweight thread to match or contrast the fabric

tools and supplies

- Serger (optional)

Cut

1. Cut the fabric into an 18" x 18" square.

2. Repeat Step 1 for each napkin to be made.

Press

1. With the wrong side of the fabric facing up, place the fabric on a line of the pressing surface. Fold back one edge by ½" and press in place.

2. Repeat Step 1 for all of the edges of all of the napkins.

3. Fold back another ½" of fabric. Press in place.

4. Repeat Step 3 for all of the edges of all of the napkins. A total of 1" of fabric should be folded under for each side of each napkin.

5. Unfold the pressed edges at one corner. Fold back a 90-degree triangle on the 1" intersection of the pressed lines.

6. Trim away about ⅝" of the triangle. Fold the remaining ⅜" of fabric in.

7. Refold the sides to form a perfect miter at each corner.

8. Slip fusible web between the layers of fabric.

9. Iron the fabric to fuse the hem. Follow the manufacturer's directions.

10. Repeat Steps 1 through 9 for each edge of each napkin.

tip

A spray fabric protector will help dining accessories, such as napkins, table runners and bread basket liners, look their best longer. Before protecting fabric, always test a scrap first. If the test run works well, treat fabric following the manufacturer's directions. Always work in a well-ventilated space.

Autumn Leaves Napkin Rings

Autumn Leaves Napkin Rings.

Add the finishing touch to a festive autumn table display when you wrap these napkin rings around the coordinating fall print napkins shown on page 42.

Each napkin ring is made of a strip of the solid fabric with a leaf attached to hold it in place. Backing is added to individual leaves, which are cut from a large-scale fall print fabric, and the leaves' veins are stitched with decorative thread.

materials

fabric

- ¼ yd. solid or sateen fabric (for rings and backing fabric for leaves)
- ¼ yd. large-scale leaf print fabric

notions

- Scraps of batting to fill leaves
- Silk or rayon thread to contrast leaf fabric
- Spool of thread to match napkin ring fabric
- Roll of ½" wide fusible web

tools and supplies

- Small dowel or fabric turning tool

Cut

1. Cut one 2½" x 14" strip from the solid fabric.

2. Cut out one leaf shape, leaving an extra ³⁄₁₆" of fabric around the printed outline.

3. Cut a square from the backing fabric that is ½" larger on all sides than the leaf cut in Step 2.

4. Repeat Steps 1 through 3 for each napkin ring.

Mark

1. With right sides together, fold the 2½" x 14" strip in half lengthwise.

2. Lay the folded strip on a cutting mat.

3. Mark each end at a 45-degree angle. Starting ¼" from the end, draw the line from the fold toward the raw edge.

Sew and Fuse

1. Using thread that matches the fabric, stitch the ends and about 4" of the long side on each end of the ring.

2. Use a scissors to trim each end ¼" away from the stitching.

3. Turn the strip right side out. Use a dowel or turning tool to help persuade the points out.

4. Press the strip, folding the raw edges in to form a straight edge.

5. Slip a strip of fusible web in the opening. Following the manufacturer's instructions, fuse the opening closed.

6. Repeat Steps 1 through 5 for each napkin ring.

7. Center a leaf on the backing fabric, making sure the fabrics' right sides are together.

8. Using a short stitch length, sew around the entire outline of the leaf twice.

9. Trim ⅛" outside the line of stitching around the leaf. Clip every ¼" around the edge, but avoid clipping the line of stitching. Make notches in the deep inner curves of the leaves.

10. Make a 1" slit in the center of the backing fabric.

11. Turn the leaf right side out through the slit.

12. Cut a layer of batting to match each leaf shape.

13. Stuff the batting into the leaf through the slit. The slit does not need to be stitched closed, because it won't be seen once the leaf is attached to the fabric ring.

14. Use a decorative thread to stitch over the veins of the leaves.

Assemble

1. Lay the napkin ring flat.

2. Fold the napkin into the shape you desire. We overlapped the back edges of the napkin.

3. Center the napkin on the ring. Fold the ends around the napkin, and overlap them evenly in the front.

4. Place a pin at the point where the two sides cross. Slip the napkin out.

5. Sew a leaf to the center of the ring by hand.

Autumn Leaves Bread Basket Liner

Autumn Leaves Bread Basket Liner, 20" x 20".

Autumn Leaves

Create this liner to fit your favorite basket for serving hot breads or buns. It displays the fall print fabric and has leaf shapes quilted on the solid border. The measurements given will work for a 9" to 10" round basket; adjust the measurements according to the size of your basket. These liners also make quick and thoughtful hostess gifts.

materials

fabric

- ⅔ yd. fall print fabric
- ¼ yd. solid fabric

notions

- Batting scraps
- Lightweight thread to match the solid fabric
- Roll of ½" wide fusible web

Cut

1. Cut two 17" x 17" pieces from the fall print fabric.

2. Cut four 2¼" x 17" strips from the solid fabric.

3. Cut four 2¼" x 20½" strips from the solid fabric.

4. Use the Bread Basket Liner pattern as a guide to cut four pieces of batting.

Sew

1. Sew two of the shorter strips to opposing sides on one square of the fall print fabric. Press the seams open.

2. Repeat Step 1 for the second fall print fabric square.

3. Sew two of the remaining strips to the opposite sides of the same fall print fabric square. Press the seams open.

4. Repeat Step 3 for the second square.

5. Place the squares right sides together. Sew around the edge of the squares, leaving an 8" opening along one side.

6. Place one of the batting pieces at each corner. Stitch each piece in place on the line of stitching already there.

7. Turn the square right side out. Press it along the edges.

8. Turn the edges of the opening under, forming a straight edge all along that side. Press.

9. Slip a strip of fusible web in the opening. Fuse it closed according to the manufacturer's directions.

Mark and Quilt

1. Trace four copies of the design onto tracing paper according to the marking suggestions in Basic Techniques.

2. Sew a line of stitching in the seam where the two fabrics meet.

3. Pin a paper design on each corner.

4. Stitch the leaf shapes, following the quilting sequence for the leaf design as given in the Autumn Leaves Place Mats project.

5. Carefully remove the paper.

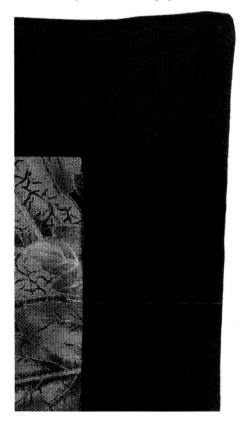

Autumn Leaves Wall Quilt

Autumn Leaves Wall Quilt, 11" x 26".

This wall quilt adds a colorful touch to the dining room wall or gives a warm welcome to guests as they step into your foyer. The fall print fabric is used for border leaf designs that are quilted in separate panes of one solid piece of fabric. Add several of the free-falling fabric leaves for a whimsical look. You can hang it vertically or horizontally to fit your space and your taste.

materials

fabric

- ¼ yd. fall print for border
- ⅓ yd. sateen or other solid fabric for quilted center and binding
- ¼ yd. fabric, either in the same fall print used on the border or in a contrasting fabric for backing

notions

- 15" x 30" piece of batting
- Lightweight thread to match the solid fabric for quilting the leaf designs
- Smoke-colored invisible thread for quilting the print fabric
- Lightweight thread for bobbin to match to the backing fabric

optional embellishments

- Free-falling leaves cut from fabric
- Scraps of batting
- Enough backing fabric for free-falling leaves
- Silk or rayon thread for stitching the veins

Cut

1. Cut one 6" x 21" piece from the solid fabric.

2. Cut two 4½" x 21" pieces from the fall print fabric for the side strips.

3. Cut two 4½" x 14" pieces from the fall print fabric for the top and bottom strips.

4. Cut one 14" x 29" piece from the backing fabric.

5. Cut one 14" x 29" piece from the batting.

6. Cut enough 2¼" wide bias strips from the solid fabric to make 84" of double-fold binding.

Sew

1. Sew the side strips to the center panel.

2. Press the seams open.

3. Sew on the top and bottom strips.

4. Press the seams open.

Mark

1. Copy the Autumn Leaves design from the pattern pullout sheet.

2. Tape the pattern to a hard surface or light box if necessary to see the pattern lines through the fabric.

3. With a water-erasable marker, draw a line on the solid fabric all the way around the piece, ½" in from the seam.

4. Draw the four 4½" squares, leaving ½" of space between them.

5. Center each square over a leaf, then trace the leaf outline and veins in each square. Remember to orientate the leaves to create either a vertical or horizontal wall quilt.

Quilt

1. Assemble the layers for quilting. See Basic Techniques for details.

2. Pin baste. Avoid placing pins on the stitching lines.

3. Using lightweight thread that matches the solid fabric, quilt in the ditch of the seam between the two fabrics.

4. Quilt the outlines of the squares and the leaves. If desired, fill the background with stippling.

5. With invisible thread in the top of the machine and lightweight thread in the bobbin to match the backing fabric, quilt the leaf fabric on the printed outlines and vein details. Fill the space evenly to the edge of the fabric.

Finish

1. When quilting is complete, wet the entire piece with cold water to remove markings.

2. Lay the piece flat to dry.

3. Lay the dried wall quilt on a flat surface. Trim the piece an even amount on all sides so it measures 11" x 26".

4. Attach the bias binding. Refer to Finishing Touches for additional information.

5. If desired, add the free-falling leaves to the quilt. Follow the instructions included in the Autumn Leaves Napkin Rings project.

Optional Embellishments

1. Attach several falling leaves to one or two corners of the piece.

2. Add a rod pocket to the back side of the quilt, along the top edge. See Finishing Touches for instructions.

This project also can be used as a table runner.

Autumn Leaves Coasters

Autumn Leaves Coaster A, 4½" to 5" in diameter.

Where are those coasters when you need them? Never wonder again if you make some of these cute accent pieces. These coasters make great additions to your autumn table ensemble, or use them all season long for mugs or glasses. Get a custom look by mixing or matching the three different designs offered.

Coaster A

Circles cut from a fall print fabric are quilted and trimmed with contrasting solid-fabric binding to create the coasters for this set. These coasters are a really quick project that's perfect to accompany a nice bottle of wine or a set of coffee mugs. What could make a nicer hostess gift?

Follow the outlines and quilt a scrap piece of fall print fabric, cut out circles and add a binding. Fussy cut each shape to get the best leaf designs centered on the coasters. Use an object that is a 4½" to 5" circular shape, such as a glass or plastic container, as a guide for cutting.

---

materials (for four coasters)

fabric

- ¼ yd. fall print fabric for top and backing
- ½ yd. solid fabric for bias binding

notions

- ¼ yd. thin batting
- Lightweight thread to match the binding fabric
- Invisible thread for quilting the print fabric

Cut

1. Cut one 6" x 24" piece from the fall print fabric.

2. Cut one 6" x 24" piece for the backing from the same print or your choice of contrasting fabric.

3. Cut one 6" x 24" piece of batting.

4. From a contrasting solid fabric, cut four strips that each are 1¼" wide and 20" long to make the single-fold bias binding.

Make sure you use a thin, flat batting to avoid bulk. Cut the bias strips 1¼" wide and apply them as a single-fold binding.

Quilt

1. Assemble the layers for quilting.

2. Pin baste the layers in place. Avoid placing pins on the outlines of the printed leaves.

3. Use the smoke-colored invisible thread in the top of your machine, and use a lightweight thread that matches the backing fabric in the bobbin. Make a practice sample to adjust the tension.

4. Follow the printed outline of the leaves, their veins and any other details to evenly distribute the quilting over the surface of the coaster. The quilting should cover the piece all the way to the outer edges.

Finish

1. When quilting is complete, trim the piece by laying it on a cutting mat and trimming it into squares or circles.

2. Attach the bias binding; refer to Finishing Touches for more directions on binding.

3. Spray the finished project with a fabric protector to help keep stains off of the coasters.

Autumn Leaves Coaster B, 4½" x 4½".

Coaster B

Here is a simply elegant design that uses squares cut from a solid fabric and quilted with one of four different leaf designs. Trim them with matching binding or try a set using a contrasting solid or print fabric.

---

materials (for four coasters)

fabric

- ½ yd. solid fabric for top, backing and bias binding

notions

- ¼ yd. thin batting
- Lightweight thread to match the fabric, or invisible thread

---

Cut

1. Cut two 6" x 24" pieces from the solid fabric.

2. Cut one 6" x 24" piece of batting.

3. Cut four 1¼" x 22" strips from the solid fabric for the single-fold bias binding.

Mark

1. Copy the patterns identified as Autumn Leaves from the paper pullout in the back of the book. Tape them to a hard surface, or use a light box if necessary.

2. Fold the solid fabric in half, then in half again. Gently crease the fabric into four 6" sections.

3. Center one square section of fabric over one of the paper designs. Tape it in place.

4. Using a water-soluble marking pen, carefully trace the outline of the leaf on the square. Be as accurate as possible.

5. Repeat Steps 3 and 4 until you have marked each of the patterns onto the fabric.

Quilt

1. Assemble the layers for quilting.

2. Pin baste the layers for quilting; see Basic Techniques for details. Avoid placing pins on the outlines of the leaves.

3. Thread the machine with lightweight thread that matches the color of the fabric.

4. Study the quilting design. Complete a practice sample to familiarize yourself with the pattern and ensure your machine's settings are correct. Refer to Basic Techniques for additional information.

5. Follow the printed outline of the leaves and their veins. If desired, the background can be filled with tiny stippling, which should fill the space to the outline of the squares.

Finish

1. When quilting is complete, wet the entire piece with cold water to remove markings. Lay the piece flat to dry.

2. Trim the dry piece into the 4½" coaster squares.

3. Attach the bias binding; refer to Finishing Touches for instructions.

4. Use a fabric protector to help keep any stains off of the coasters.

✗ tip

The coasters are small, and individually cut shapes may be difficult to hold onto during the quilting process. Leave them attached in one larger piece, then trim them to the correct size once the quilting is completed.

Autumn Leaves Coaster C, 4½" x 4½".

 Cut out individual leaf shapes and fuse them to a circle or square base of solid fabric using paper-backed fusible web. A decorative buttonhole stitch could be used to cover the raw edge of the leaf in contrasting thread. Adjust the coaster size to the size of the leaf that is being applied, if necessary.

For Coaster C, individual leaf shapes cut from print fabric are fused to squares of solid-colored fabric. Trim the coasters with a solid binding that matches or contrasts the coasters, or use the fall print.

---

materials (for four coasters)

fabric

- ⅓ yd. solid fabric for top, backing and bias binding
- ¼ yd. fall leaf fabric, or a large enough scrap to cut out four complete leaves

notions

- ¼ yd. thin batting
- Lightweight thread to match or contrast fabric, or use invisible thread
- ¼ yd. paper-backed fusible web

Cut

1. Cut two 6" x 24" pieces from the solid-colored fabric.

2. Cut one 6" x 24" piece from the batting.

3. Cut four 1¼" x 24" strips to make the single-fold bias binding.

Fuse

1. Fold the solid fabric in half, then in half again. Gently crease the fabric into four 6" sections.

2. Apply paper-backed fusible web to the back side of the leaf print fabric, then cut out four complete leaves.

3. Fuse one leaf in the center of each square. Follow the manufacturer's instructions.

4. Use a decorative stitch and heavier thread to overcast the raw edges of the leaves, if desired.

Mark and Quilt

1. Draw a 4½" to 5" circle or square around each leaf. Use a water-soluble marker.

2. Assemble the layers for quilting, and pin them in place. Straight pins will work fine for this tiny project. Refer to Basic Techniques for more information.

3. Using invisible thread in the top of the machine and lightweight thread in the bobbin to match the backing fabric, quilt on the leaf fabric, going around the outline of the leaf. Quilt on the vein lines and any other details that should be highlighted.

4. If desired, stipple the background. Use the same thread as was used for the leaves or choose a light-weight thread to match the solid fabric.

Finish

1. Trim into individual coasters.

2. Apply binding to each coaster; refer to the instructions for binding in Finishing Touches.

Variations

Wondering how to put a different twist on the projects in this chapter? Try these variations to customize the projects to fit your taste.

Grape Table Runner, 16" x 26", shown with Autumn Leaves Wine Bottle Bag with Leaf Tie Band closure.

Grape Table Runner

This simple table runner uses the leaf border quilting design. A large-scale fabric featuring bunches of grapes was chosen for the theme fabric. Quilted rows of leaves create contrasting borders that are finished with dramatically-colored lace. Make your own hand-painted lace trim using the directions in Finishing Touches.

You can follow dimensions for the Autumn Leaves Table Runner, or you can customize the project by sizing it to fit your furniture. Cut a piece of solid fabric for the band, and cut the lace the same width. Quilt the design following the directions for the Autumn Leaves Table Runner, and add the lace for an elegant finishing touch.

Autumn Leaves Wine Bottle Bag With Leaf Tie Band

Use your scraps to stitch up a coordinating gift bag for a bottle of wine. Create a tie band following the Autumn Leaves Napkin Ring pattern.

Autumn Leaves **Potholders**

Autumn Leaves Potholders, 7"x 7".

This lovely pair of Potholders uses the same quilting design as the Autumn Leaves Heat-Resistant Trivet. Use the heat-resistant batting and backing fabric to offer protection from hot dishes.

Follow the same plan as in the directions for the larger trivet, except change the cutting size for all layers to 11" x 11". Use the double-square outline as your cutting line, omitting the border space around the design. Follow the quilting and finishing directions provided for the trivet.

The heart has been used as a traditional symbol of love and romance. The decorative projects featured in this chapter — a pillow, a runner with hand-painted lace, a framed quilted heart design, a quilted book cover and a bed tote — will enrich any bedroom with elegance. Each creation features a heart design quilted on richly colored sateen.

Heart's Desire

Heart's Desire Pillow

Heart's Desire Pillow, 14" x 14".

Heart's Desire

The heart design featured on this pillow is in its purest form. This project is a great way to practice your skill and become familiar with the shapes used for the design before you try it for a project that is scaled down to an intricate size. Stitch the design, then add an elegant touch with some pearls and fancy trim. Find out for yourself how really easy it is to make this complicated-looking project.

materials

fabric

- ½ yd. solid fabric for top and pillow back
- ½ yd. lining fabric used for quilting (will not be seen)

notions

- ½ yd. batting
- Lightweight thread to match top fabric
- 2 yd. manufactured cording
- 14" pillow form
- Beads or pearls (optional; the piece shown used 125 pearls)

tools and supplies

- Zipper foot for sewing machine
- Beading needle (optional)

Cut

1. Cut one 18" x 18" piece of fabric for the top of the quilted pillow.

2. Cut one 18" x 18" piece of batting.

3. Cut one 18" x 18" piece of lining fabric.

4. Cut two 9" x 15" pieces of the solid fabric for the overlapping pillow back.

Quilt

1. Assemble the layers for quilting as directed in Basic Techniques.

2. Study the quilting sequence. Complete a practice sample to familiarize yourself with the pattern and to ensure your machine's settings are correct. Refer to Basic Techniques for additional information.

3. Start at the point indicated on the pattern, and stitch the inner heart outline. Stop with the needle down.

4. Stitch all of the lines that make up the decorative design within the heart. They all are connected, and all can be stitched with the same thread.

5. Move to the nearest grid line, and begin filling in the grid. Travel along the outline of the heart to get to the next grid line. Secure the thread when the grid is completely filled.

6. Begin a new line of stitching. Complete the outer heart outline, and secure the thread.

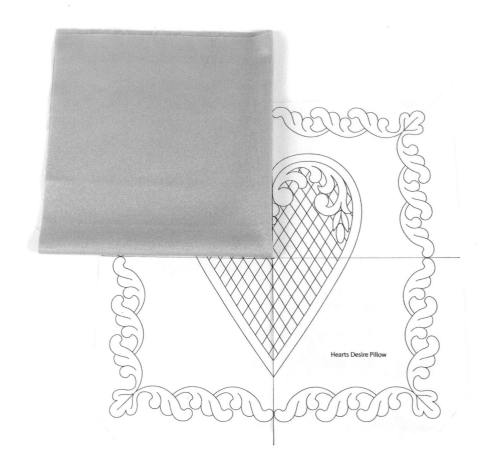

Hearts Desire Pillow

Mark

1. Trace the design identified as Heart's Desire Pillow. Tape the pattern to a hard surface, or use a light box if necessary.

2. Fold the top fabric in half in both directions and lightly crease it. Position this creased line over the dotted line of the paper pattern, and securely tape the fabric in place.

3. Using a water-soluble marker, accurately trace the design.

4. Draw a 14" x 14" square to indicate the outer edge of the design area of the piece.

tip

When working with sateen, remember to mark the top edges of the fabric to keep the sheen of the fabric running in the same direction.

7. Stitch the entire border using one thread. Begin where indicated on the pattern, and follow the inner scalloped line made by the connecting motifs to the corner. Fill in the veins of the corner section, and stitch all the way around the four sides and back to the starting point.

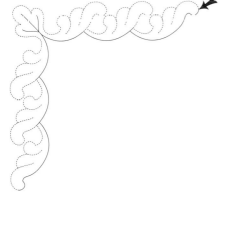

8. Move right onto the outer line that completes the motif shapes. When stitching, your path may retrace segments of the lines.

9. If you wish, stipple the background, filling the entire area around the heart and just past the marked outline.

Finish

1. Remove the quilting lines with cold water. Smooth out the piece, and dry it flat.

2. Trim all four sides of the piece evenly to create a 15" x 15" square.

3. Attach the beads or pearls to the heart with hand stitching. Secure your stitches on the back.

4. Add cording to the pillow. Refer to the directions in Finishing Touches.

5. Finish the back of the pillow. Refer to the directions in Finishing Touches.

Heart's Desire Dresser Runner

Heart's Desire Dresser Runner, 11" x 22", excluding lace trim.

Heart's Desire

This runner showcases the Heart's Desire quilting pattern that repeats elements used for the other projects in Heart's Desire. For this pattern, the design is arranged in a rectangular shape that is filled with a diamond grid.

You can coordinate this runner to match your decor by trimming it with hand-painted lace; follow the directions in Finishing Touches to paint your own lace. When choosing the lace, consider the size of the motifs compared with the finished width of the runner.

materials

fabric

- 1 yd. sateen or solid fabric for the top, backing and binding

notions

- 15" x 26" piece of batting
- Lightweight thread to match the fabric
- 24" flat lace made of rayon or cotton/rayon blend

tools and supplies

- Zipper foot for sewing machine
- Acrylic-based fabric paints to coordinate with fabric used in project
- Paintbrush

Cut

1. Cut two 15" x 26" pieces from the solid fabric, one for the top and one for the backing.

2. Cut one 15" x 26" piece from the batting.

3. Cut enough 2¼" wide binding strips from the solid fabric to total 76" in length.

4. Cut two 11" pieces of prepared lace.

Paint (optional)

1. If desired, hand-paint the lace trim. See Finishing Touches for instructions to paint lace.

2. Let the lace dry completely before using it for the project.

Mark

1. Copy or trace the Heart's Desire Dresser Runner pattern, and tape it to a hard surface.

2. Fold the top fabric in half, then in half again. Lightly crease the fabric.

3. Center the fabric over the paper design and tape it securely in place.

4. Trace the design onto the fabric using a water-soluble marker.

Quilt

1. Assemble the layers for quilting. Refer to Basic Techniques for more detailed instructions.

2. Study the quilting sequence. Complete a practice sample to familiarize yourself with the pattern and ensure your machine's settings are correct. Refer to Basic Techniques for additional information.

3. Secure the thread where indicated by the arrow on the pattern.

4. Begin quilting, following the line completely around the design to a point just past the starting point. Stop with the needle down.

5. Stitch the curving lines that make up the main design on one end of the runner.

6. Follow the straight inner line to the other end of the design. Complete the curved design at

that end, and stitch your way back to the first end on the inner line. Stop with the needle down.

7. Fill in the grid. Follow the suggestions in Basic Techniques to complete the grid and secure the thread.

8. Fill in the background with stippling just past the outline of the runner.

tip

The dimensions for this project can be adjusted slightly by adding to or eliminating the space surrounding the central design. Or, you can use the information in Basic Techniques as a guide to alter the size significantly to fit any furniture piece. Remember to adjust the fabric and lace amounts if you change the size of the runner.

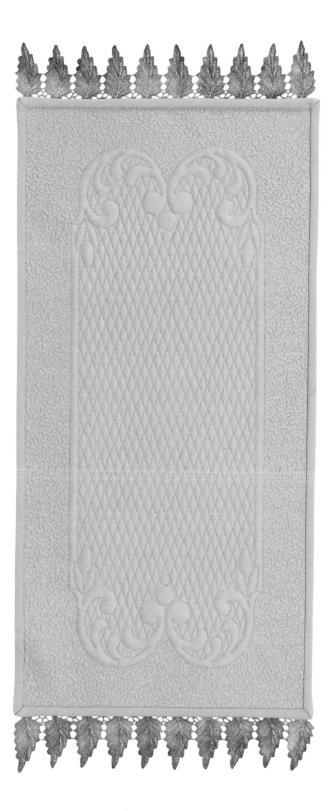

Finish

1. Remove the marking lines with cold water. Lay the piece flat to dry.

2. Trim the runner to 11" x 22".

3. Sew on the binding. Refer to the binding directions in Finishing Touches. Slipstitch the binding edge to the back side of the quilt by hand.

4. If you are adding lace, pin each piece along the ends of the runner. Hand sew the lace to the back of the binding, hiding the edge of the lace behind the binding.

Heart's Desire Frame with Quilted Heart, 3⅝" x 5⅝" as shown in the frame.

Purchase a pretty frame and stitch this design on sateen to make a unique display for one of your treasures, such as a piece of keepsake jewelry, a pin or an antique button. The center of the heart is the perfect setting to enjoy your "unburied" treasure.

The frame shown has a 3⅝" x 5⅝" opening. You can choose a frame with a similarly sized opening, or you can adjust the design to fit by adding more space around the heart. Before you start cutting any fabric, make sure you measure the opening of the frame from the front; you will use these dimensions to compute the cutting size for your fabric.

materials

fabric

- 8" x 10" scrap of solid-colored fabric
- 8" x 10" scrap of fabric for backing

notions

- 8" x 10" scrap of batting
- Lightweight thread to match the fabric

tools and supplies

- Manufactured picture frame with 3⅝" x 5⅝" opening
- Acid-free mat board
- Acid-free mounting tape, 1" wide
- Pin, button, jewelry or other treasure to highlight in the heart
- 1" of ¼" wide ribbon (optional)

Measure

1. Measure the width of the frame opening. Add 4" to that dimension to compute the final width for your fabric.

2. Measure the height of the frame opening. Add 4" to compute the final height for your fabric.

Cut

1. Cut one piece of solid-colored fabric to the dimensions you calculated in the Measure steps to serve as the top piece of the design. The fabric shown in the project is 7⅝" x 9⅝".

2. Cut one piece of batting the same size as the top piece of fabric.

3. Cut one piece of backing fabric the same size as the top piece of fabric. The backing fabric will not be seen.

Mark

1. Copy the Heart's Desire Framed Heart design from the pattern pullout. Adjust the size to fit your project's dimensions.

2. Tape the copied pattern to a hard surface or light box to see the lines through the fabric.

3. Fold the fabric in half lengthwise and widthwise, and gently crease those folds.

4. Center the fabric over the pattern. Tape it securely in place.

5. Trace the Framed Heart pattern onto the fabric. This is an intricate pattern, so use as fine a line as possible to trace the pattern. Or, try the Trace and Stitch method detailed in Basic Techniques.

6. Center the frame opening over the heart, and mark an outline that will indicate where the stippled background should end.

Quilt

1. Assemble the layers for quilting. Refer to Basic Techniques for more information.

2. Study the quilting sequence. Complete a practice sample to familiarize yourself with the pattern and ensure your machine's settings are correct. Refer to Basic Techniques for additional information.

3. Start quilting at the point indicated on the pattern. Stitch the inner heart outline and the decorative design lines within the heart.

4. With the same thread, move right to the nearest grid line. Fill in the grid; re-stitch the outlines of the heart to get to the next line of the grid. Secure the thread.

5. Stitch the outer heart outline.

6. Stipple the background if desired, bumping up against the heart outline and filling beyond the frame opening.

Finish

1. Remove the quilting lines with cold water, and the lay the piece flat to dry.

2. Hand stitch the treasure to the point of the heart, securing your stitches on the back.

Frame

1. Measure the frame opening from the back side. This measurement should be about ½" larger than the front opening because of the ridge inside the frame opening.

2. Mark the center point of the frame on all four sides.

8. Fold the top fabric to the back. Securely tape the edge with mounting tape.

9. Work from opposite sides to tape the rest of the fabric in place. Gently pull the fabric taut while pressing the tape down.

10. Insert the artwork into the frame opening, then close the back of the frame and display as desired.

3. Cut a piece of acid-free mat board that measures slightly less than the back opening. Mark horizontal and vertical centerlines on the backside.

5. Trim away the excess batting and backing. Trim the front layer so it measures 1" larger than the cardboard on all sides.

6. Clip away the corners to avoid bulk. Cut on the diagonal.

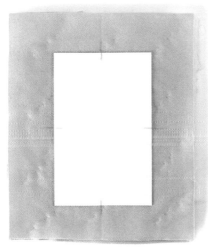

4. Use a water-soluble marker to draw the centerlines of the heart on the front and back of the quilted piece. These lines will help you to center the heart in the frame. Draw the outline of the mat board on the back side of the quilted piece as a guide for cutting away unnecessary layers.

7. Center the artwork over the mat board. Make sure the heart is straight.

⚡tips

• When using small, intricate designs that are more challenging to mark and stitch, try the Trace and Stitch Marking Method detailed in Basic Techniques.

• If the item you wish to display is a pin that you would like to be able to remove from the frame, sew a small loop of ¼" wide ribbon to the heart and pin it to the loop using the pin back, as shown in the photo below.

Frame with Quilted Heart 85

Heart's Desire Quilted Book Cover

Heart's Desire Quilted Book Cover, 4¼" x 6¼" as shown, but can be made to fit any size book.

For this beautiful project, coordinate the décor of your bedroom with a quilted cover for your journal, Bible or any favorite book you might keep close at hand for bedtime reading. Choose a solid cotton or sateen fabric to highlight the quilted heart motif for the front cover.

The pattern can be adjusted to fit any size book. The construction is based on the grocery-bag book covers I made for my schoolbooks when I was a child.

---

materials
fabric

- ⅓ yd. solid fabric for top, flaps and lining
- ¼ yd. backing fabric for quilting (fabric won't be seen)

notions

- ½ yd. batting
- Lightweight thread to match the top fabric

Measure

1. Measure the book's width, height and spine thickness.

2. Calculate the total book width by adding the width of the book front, the width of the back and the thickness of the spine.

3. Add 4" to the total book width calculated in Step 2. This is your total fabric width.

4. Calculate the total book height by adding the height of the book front and the height of the book back.

5. Add 4" to the total book height calculated in Step 4. This is your total fabric height.

5. Position the fabric over the paper design so that the heart is where you want it on the front cover panel. The heart motif on the cover is designed to be slightly off center.

6. Mark the pattern with a water-soluble marker. Do not mark stippling lines. Use a light touch and as fine a line as possible when tracing this intricate design. This may be a time to try the optional Trace and Stitch marking method detailed in Basic Techniques.

Cut

1. Cut two pieces of sateen to the dimensions you calculated in Steps 3 and 5. The fabric will be the top and inside lining.

2. Cut one piece of backing fabric the same size as the top.

3. Cut one piece of batting the same size as the top.

4. Cut two pieces of sateen for the flaps that are 5½" wide by the heigh calculated in the measure steps.

Mark

1. Use a water-soluble marker to draw the outline of the book onto the fabric.

2. Draw in the lines that indicate the spine and front and back covers. This will help you place the quilting design in your space.

3. Copy the Heart's Desire Quilted Book Cover design from the pattern pullout.

4. Tape the paper pattern to a hard surface; use a light box if needed.

✂ Create a custom fit

When measuring your book to calculate the cover size, remember to consider whether the bound book is padded. You will need to increase the amount of space around the outside sewing line to allow for any padding. A good way to know how the cover will fit your book is to construct a practice cover before you cut your final fabric.

You may need to adjust the quilting design if your book varies substantially from the size of the book used in this project. Refer to Basic Techniques for more information. You also can increase or decrease the space around the design to fit your book if it is close to the size of the book we used.

Any easy rule of thumb to remember: Add 2" of fabric to each side of the measurement to get your finished cutting size.

Quilt

1. When the marking is complete, assemble the layers for quilting. Refer to Basic Techniques for details.

2. Study the quilting sequence following the techniques described in Basic Techniques. Complete a practice sample to familiarize yourself with the pattern and to ensure your machine's settings are correct.

3. Stitch the inner heart shape, starting at the point indicated on the pattern.

4. Stitch the inner heart outline and the curvilinear design lines within the heart.

5. Stitch the outer heart outline.

6. Stitch the five lines that connect with the heart and the two pairs of parallel lines that border the heart design.

7. Fill in the remaining book cover with tiny stippling.

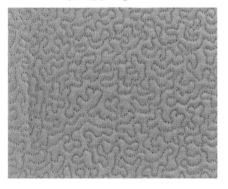

Finish

1. Remove markings with cold water. Lay the piece flat to dry.

2. Lay the book out flat on top of the dry quilted piece. Draw an outline around the book.

3. Trim the top of the piece at least ½" larger than the outline. Increase that amount if your book is padded or has thick cover material. Be generous with these measurements. It is better at this point for the cover to be too large and for you to have to re-sew it than to have it too tight to fit the book.

4. Fold the flap pieces in half lengthwise, with wrong sides together. Press the flaps.

5. Layer the piece as follows:
   • Quilted top, right-side up;
   • One flap at each end, with raw edges matched to the top edges;
   • Lining, right side down, on top of the stack.

6. Pin the layers together, matching raw edges.

7. Make a mark to indicate the space at the bottom of the cover that will not be stitched so you can turn the cover right-side out.

8. Stitch ¼" outside the book outline around the cover. Do not stitch between the flaps along the bottom edge.

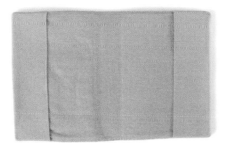

9. Turn the cover right-side out.

10. Place the cover on the book for a trial fitting. It will fit better when you trim away the excess batting and corners, but this is the best way to test whether you will need to make any adjustments.

11. When you are satisfied that the cover fits properly, reinforce the seams, especially at the corners.

12. Trim away the excess batting from the seams. Clip the corners on the diagonal, but avoid cutting too close to the stitching.

13. Turn the cover right-side out.

14. Press the bulky seams with your fingers.

15. Pin closed the opening along the bottom edge. Fold the edges under in a straight line.

16. Use a blind stitch to sew the opening along the bottom edge closed.

Heart's Desire Bed Tote, 11" x 21".

You never will misplace your eyeglasses or TV remote between the sheets again with this bed tote. Here's handy storage right where you need it. The quilted background layer slips between the mattress and box spring, and two roomy pockets keep your bedtime favorites within easy reach. Revisit the Heart's Desire design, which is quilted on the beautiful outer pocket. This useful project is so pretty and so simple to make that you will want to have one for yourself and make another for a friend.

materials
fabric

- 1¼ yd. solid fabric for pockets and the binding
- ⅔ yd. print fabric for background and backing
- ⅓ yd. any cotton fabric for the lining

notions

- 11" hand-painted lace
- 11" ribbon trim
- ½ yd. batting
- Lightweight thread to match the solid fabric
- Invisible or lightweight thread to quilt the print

tools and supplies

- Acrylic paint
- Paintbrush
- Walking foot for a sewing machine

Cut

1. Cut two 12" x 22" pieces from the print fabric for the background and backing.

2. Cut one 12" x 12" piece of batting (pocket) and one 12" x 22" piece of batting (backing).

3. Cut one 12" x 12" piece (quilted front pocket) and one 12" x 22" piece from the solid fabric for (back pocket).

4. Cut one 12" x 12" piece from the lining fabric.

5. Cut enough 2¼" wide strips from the solid fabric to make 80" of double-fold bias binding.

Paint (optional)

1. If desired, hand-paint the lace you will use for the project. See Finishing Touches for details.

2. Let the lace dry before using it in the project.

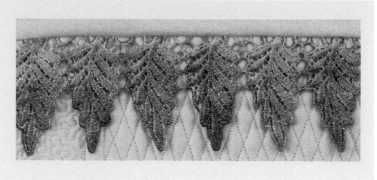

Mark and Quilt Front Pocket

1. Copy one half of the Heart's Desire Dresser Runner design from the pattern pullout with rounded corners.

2. Trace the design onto the front pocket fabric.

3. Layer the pocket fabric, batting and lining.

4. Follow the instructions for quilting the design as given in the Heart's Desire Dresser Runner project. Use lightweight thread to match the fabric.

Background Piece

1. Layer the background fabric, batting and backing.

2. Quilt the layers with invisible or lightweight thread that matches the fabric. Meander or outline the designs, stitching out to the edge of the fabric.

Back Pocket

1. Fold the rear pocket fabric in half horizontally. Sew a strip of ribbon trim ⅜" down from the fold.

2. Trim the pocket to 9" x 11". Round the bottom corners according to the pattern.

Front Pocket

1. Copy the half of the Heart's Desire Table Runner pattern with the rounded corners from the pattern pullout in the back of the book. Tape it to a hard surface.

2. Center the fabric over the design and trace it with a water-soluble marker.

3. Layer the pocket front, batting and lining.

4. Follow the instructions for quilting the design as given in the Heart's Desire Dresser Runner project. Use lightweight thread to match the fabric.

5. Sew a piece of lace ¼" from the top edge of the front pocket.

6. Sew a strip of the bias binding across the top edge, covering the top edge of the lace.

7. Fold the binding over the edge. Hand stitch the binding to the back side of the pocket.

Assemble and Finish

1. Layer the quilted backing piece, the rear pocket and the front pocket. Make sure the bottom and side edges match.

2. Trim all the layers to 11" x 21", rounding the bottom corners.

3. Pin the raw edge of the binding to match the raw edges of all of the layers.

4. Use the walking foot to add the bias binding to the outer edge. Turn the binding to the back and whipstitch it to the back edge of the tote.

Variations

Stretch your imagination and create different projects using the various Heart's Desire patterns. Here are two ideas to get you started.

Heart's Desire Wall Hanging

Use the pillow design to make a wall hanging. Add a decorator print from your decor to use as a wide border.

Heart's Desire Covered Box

Use the tiny heart pattern to create a quilted top panel for a fabric-covered box.

We look to tradition for the inspiration for these quick and easy home-decorating projects. The quilting designs evolve from classically based patterns seen on ceramic tiles from the past. They are quite easy to stitch, even if they don't seem so at first glance. Choose several wonderful fabrics and build you room decor around these projects. The projects feature simple construction techniques. Use your creative touch to enhance them with embellishments. Let your imagination take over, and think outside the box. Have fun trying something new!

Classic Tiles

Classic Tiles Table Mat, 16" x 24".

This sophisticated mat is quilted on solid sateen to add a touch of elegance to your room. The simple pattern blends a classic diamond grid with a softly sculptured center design and border. Study the design to see how it has been altered to make the coordinating Classic Tiles Pillows and Coasters, which finish the coordinated look.

materials

fabric

- 1¼ yd. solid fabric for top, backing and binding

notions

- ⅔ yd. batting
- Lightweight thread to match the solid fabric

Cut

1. Cut two 20" x 28" pieces from the solid fabric for the top and the backing.

2. Cut one 20" x 28" piece from the batting.

3. Cut enough 2¼" wide bias strips from the solid fabric to make 96" of double-fold binding.

Mark

1. Copy the Classic Tiles Table Mat pattern.

2. Tape the pattern to a hard surface, or light box if necessary.

3. Fold your fabric in half and then in half again to create quarters. Lightly crease it in both directions.

4. Match the creases to the dotted lines on the pattern.

5. Tape the fabric in place.

6. Trace the quilting lines onto the fabric. Use a ruler when tracing the grid lines.

7. Draw a 16" x 24" rectangle outline to indicate where to end the stippling.

Quilt

1. Assemble the layers for quilting. Refer to Basic Techniques for details.

2. Study the Classic Tiles Table Mat design and quilting sequence; see Basic Techniques for additional information. Complete a practice sample to familiarize yourself with the pattern and to ensure your machine's settings are correct.

3. Begin quilting at the arrow. Follow the line to the center of the design.

4. Turn right to make the loop, and then stitch back to the center.

5. Follow the bottom loop and the loop on the left.

6. When you return to the center, stitch around the circle and head toward the top.

7. Complete the final long loop. Stop with the needle in the fabric just past the starting point.

8. Continue to follow all of the other curved lines that make up the central design. Work in a clockwise direction. You will need to retrace the stitching segments of those lines and the ends of the long loops.

9. When you complete the design and arrive back at the place where you began, secure your threads.

10. Stitch the line of echo quilting around the center design.

11. Move to the border. Begin as indicated on the pattern. This is the same quilting sequence that was used for the Heart's Desire Pillow project.

12. Follow the inner scalloped line made by the connecting motifs around the entire quilt and back to the starting point. Each time you reach a corner, stitch up the line and the veins of the corner, then move on to finish that scalloping line.

13. When you arrive back at your starting place, move to the outer line that completes the motifs. There will be times when you will need to stitch back over segments of the lines.

14. Move right onto the grid, pivoting or retracing lines to get to the next line until you completely fill in the grid. See Basic Techniques for helpful suggestions about how to complete the grid.

15. Stipple the area from the border design out past the marked line indicating where to stop stippling. Make sure the stippling touches the edges of the motifs and the outline.

⟡ Make a light box

Several of the projects pictured in this chapter feature dark-colored sateen, which required the use of a light box to transfer the pattern. Refer to Basic Techniques for directions to make your own large light box and for an optional method you can use to mark the designs.

Finish

1. When quilting is complete, remove markings by submerging the piece in cold water. Lay the piece flat to dry.

2. Trim the dry piece to 16" x 24".

3. Assemble the binding strips, and apply them to the piece. Refer to Finishing Touches for details on binding.

Classic Tiles **Pillows One and Two**

Classic Tiles Pillows One and Two, 16" x 16".

Try these pillow designs to accent your living room, den or bedroom. The versatility of these simple designs will blend beautifully with traditional fabrics. Or, you can try contemporary fabrics for a completely different look.

Combine floral prints, richly colored solids and manufactured trims and cording to complete your own set of these lovely pillows.

Classic Tiles Pillows One and Two

materials (for one pillow)

fabric

- ⅓ yd. sateen fabric for center of the pillow top
- ¼ yd. contrasting solid for narrow accent strips
- ½ yd. large-scale accent print fabric for wide border and backing
- 18" x 18" piece of lining fabric, which will not be seen

notions

- ½ yd. batting
- Invisible thread
- Lightweight thread to match solid fabric
- 2 yd. manufactured cording
- 16" pillow form

Cut

1. Cut one 11" x 11" piece from the sateen fabric for the center of the pillow top.

2. Cut two 1" x 11" strips from the contrasting solid fabric for the top and bottom accent borders.

3. Cut two 1" x 12" strips from the contrasting solid fabric for the side accent borders.

4. Cut two 3½" x 12" strips from the large accent print for the top and bottom wide borders.

5. Cut two 3½" x 18" strips from the accent print for the side wide borders.

6. Cut one 18" x 18" square from the lining fabric.

7. Cut one 18" x 18" square from the batting.

8. Cut two 11" x 18" pieces of print fabric for the overlapping pillow back.

Trim

1. Using a ¼" seam allowance, sew the small accent border strips to the top and bottom edges of the center square.

2. Press the seams open.

3. Sew on the small accent border side strips.

4. Press the seams open.

5. Sew on the wide top and bottom border strips.

6. Press the seams open.

7. Sew on the wide side border strips.

8. Press the seams open.

Mark

1. Copy the Classic Tiles pattern that you are using.

2. Tape the pattern to a hard surface, or a light box, if necessary. For dark fabrics, use a white marker. You also can try the alternate marking method offered in Basic Techniques.

3. Gently crease a fold in the center of the pieced top, across the width and down the length of the square.

4. Center the fabric over the paper design. Tape the fabric in place.

5. Trace the quilting lines onto the fabric using a water-soluble pen. A sharp, white water-erasable pencil may be helpful for marking dark fabrics.

Quilt

1. Assemble the layers for quilting.

2. Study the quilting sequence. Complete a practice sample to familiarize yourself with the pattern and ensure your machine's settings are correct. Refer to Basic Techniques for additional information.

3. Begin quilting following the sequence that matches the pillow that you are making.

Classic Tiles Pillow One

1. Anchor the layers by quilting in the ditch on both sides of the accent border, using invisible thread.

2. Follow the quilting sequence for the Classic Tiles Table Runner to quilt the center design.

3. Complete the double square outlines. Stitch the inner square first, starting close to a place where one of the corner designs meets that line.

4. Follow the four corner designs. Retrace the square line to get to the next corner design. The design will be complete when the central space is filled with stippling. Remember to fill in the little shield-shaped spaces that are created by the corners of the designs and to touch the edges of the designs with the stippling.

5. Move to a corner of the outer square line. Stitch around the entire square. Leave the thread in the fabric.

6. Begin stippling the background. Fill in the area from the border design just past the marked outline.

7. If desired, quilt the print fabric border. Use smoke-colored invisible thread and follow the outlines of the designs to evenly distribute the quilting throughout the border.

Classic Tiles Pillow Two

1. Study the quilting sequence. This tile design is made up of four ovals and buds, plus an eight-pointed outline. Familiarize yourself with the pattern, complete a practice sample and ensure your machine's settings are correct. Refer to Basic Techniques for additional information.

2. Anchor the layers by quilting in the ditch on both sides of the accent border.

3. Begin quilting at the bottom of the small circle in the oval design, as indicated on the pattern.

4. Stitch around the circle and up the center of the oval, making the three scallops.

5. Stitch back down the side of the oval. Stitch up the two vein lines, retrace your stitch line over each one and continue back down to the bottom.

6. Stitch back to the top of the oval.

7. Stitch down the pattern to the 2 o'clock position to complete the first oval.

8. Retrace the line back up to the point where the oval meets the bud.

9. Stitch the bud base to the point where it meets the second oval on the right.

10. Backtrack to stitch the bud. Lock your stitches where the bud connects with its base.

11. Continue around the design in the same manner until all ovals and buds are complete.

12. Stitch the two lines of the eight-pointed outline. Secure your stitches at the intersection of two points.

13. Complete the inner square line and the corner designs, ending with the thread in the fabric.

14. Fill in the central space with stippling. Remember to fill in the little shield-shaped spaces that are created by the corners of the designs, and be sure to touch the edges of the designs with the stippling.

15. Begin a new thread for the outer square line and the stippling that fills the space up to the accent strip.

16. Quilt the print border if desired, using smoke-colored invisible thread and following the outlines of the designs to evenly distribute the quilting throughout the border.

Finish

1. Remove the quilting lines by submerging the piece in cold water.

2. Smooth out the quilted piece, and let it dry flat.

3. Evenly trim all four sides of the piece to a 17" x 17" square.

4. Attach the cording and complete the two-panel pillow back. Refer to Finishing Touches for directions.

Classic Tiles Pillow Three, 14" x 14".

Don't you love pillows that have a triangular-shaped flap of fabric placed over a coordinating background? I see that empty triangle as a potential space to fill with a beautiful quilted design.

Look closely and you will see that a section of the design used for the Classic Tiles Pillow Two was used to create this three-sided design. Try the easy faux cording technique detailed in Finishing Touches; it makes finishing the pillow extra simple!

materials

fabric

- ¼ yd. sateen fabric for the triangle

- ½ yd. large-scale print fabric for top and backing

- ⅓ yd. black solid fabric for the faux cording and the narrow accent strips

- 16" x 16" square of any fabric for lining, which won't be seen

notions

- ½ yd. batting

- Lightweight thread to match the solid and the black fabric

- Smoke-colored invisible thread

- 14" pillow form

- Home decorating tassels and trims (optional)

- 2 yd. manufactured cording (optional)

- One decorative bead, any size

Cut

1. Cut two 16" x 16" pieces from the print fabric, one for the pillow front and one for the pillow back.

2. Cut one triangle that measures 16" across the top and 11" on each side from the solid fabric. I used the triangle left over from cutting binding from another project in the book. I also used the triangular shape from the Classic Tiles Long Table Runner pattern as a cutting guide.

3. Cut two 1½" x 12" strips on the straight grain of the black fabric for the accent border.

4. Cut enough 2½" wide bias strips from the black fabric to total 68" in length. These are for the faux cording.

5. Cut one 16" x 16" piece from the lining fabric for the backing layer. This fabric will not be seen.

6. Cut two 16" x 16" pieces of batting, one for the front and one for the back.

7. Cut enough 1" wide strips of batting to total 68" in length. The batting will stuff the faux cording.

Assemble

1. Fold the black accent strips in half lengthwise, with right sides out.

2. Press the fold.

3. Match the raw edge of one strip to one of the 11" sides of the triangle.

4. Using a ¼" seam allowance, sew the strip to the triangle.

5. Press the seams toward the triangle.

6. Fold under ¼" of the end of the second strip.

7. Sew the strip to the opposite side of the triangle. Line up the folded end with the first strip.

8. Press the seams toward the triangle.

Mark

1. Copy the Classic Tiles Long Table Runner pattern.

2. Tape the pattern to a hard surface, or light box if necessary.

3. Gently crease a fold down the center of the fabric triangle.

4. Tape the fabric triangle in place over the paper design.

5. Mark the quilting design.

6. Center the marked triangle on top of the print fabric square.

7. Using thread that matches the accent strip, topstitch the layers together along the outside edge of the strip.

Quilt

1. Assemble the layers for quilting as directed in Basic Techniques.

2. Use invisible thread to stitch in the ditch along both edges of the black accent strip. This will anchor the layers.

3. Use a lightweight thread that matches the fabric for the triangle to stitch the outline of the triangle ¼" inside the edge of the black strip.

4. Follow the suggestions for quilting the center of the pillow used in the Classic Tiles Pillow Two project.

5. Fill in the straight lines above the buds. Start at the top on either end, then stitch down to meet the outline of the design. Retrace the outline over to the next line, back up to the top edge. Move across the entire section in this manner.

6. Use invisible thread to quilt around the flowers and leaves of the print fabric, all the way to the outer edge.

Finish

1. Remove the quilting lines by submerging the piece in cold water. Smooth out the quilted piece, and let it dry flat.

2. Square up the quilted piece by laying it on a cutting mat. Trim the quilted piece to 16" square.

3. Follow the instructions given in Finishing Touches for finishing a Pillow with Faux Cording.

4. Embellish the pillow as desired by adding beads, tassels or decorative trims.

Classic Tiles Framed Corner Blocks, varying sizes.

This is a really quick project that makes a lovely gift.

Use the Corner Block design from the Classic Tiles group for this framed accessory. Purchase a manufactured frame, and have a mat cut to fit the frame. Cover the mat with your fabric. Stitch the design on a pretty solid fabric, and pop it in a frame.

If the size of your frame is a substantially different than ours, read the information in Basic Techniques to figure out how to adapt the pattern, then adjust the fabric cutting sizes accordingly.

materials

fabric

- ⅓ yd. solid fabric
- ⅓ yd. print fabric to cover mat
- ⅓ yd. backing fabric, which will not be seen

notions

- ⅓ yd. batting
- 24" of small-scale decorative cording
- Lightweight thread to match the solid fabric

tools and supplies

- Square frame with an 8" square opening
- 8" x 8" square of acid-free mat board, on which the quilted piece will be mounted
- Acid-free mat board, cut to fit in the frame, with a 5" square opening
- Acid-free mounting tape, ¾" to 1" wide
- Spray mounting adhesive for fabric
- Thick, tacky glue
- Razor blade knife

Cut

1. Cut one 10" x 10" piece from the solid fabric for the top.

2. Cut one 10" x 10" piece of solid fabric for the backing. This will not be seen, so any scrap fabric can be used.

3. Cut one 10" x 10" piece of batting.

Mark

1. Copy the Classic Tiles Corner Block pattern.

2. Tape the pattern to a hard surface, or light box if necessary.

3. Center the fabric square over the paper design. Tape the fabric in place.

4. Mark the pattern onto the fabric; use a water-soluble marker.

Quilt

1. Assemble the layers for quilting as directed in Basic Techniques.

2. Study the quilting sequence for the center design of the Classic Tiles Table Mat project as directed in Basic Techniques. Complete a practice sample to familiarize yourself with the pattern and ensure your machine's settings are correct. Refer to Basic Techniques for additional information.

3. With thread matching the fabric, stitch the double outline around the design to anchor the layers. Secure the thread.

4. Use the Classic Tiles Corner Block pattern and follow the quilting sequence for the center design of the Classic Table Mat project.

5. If desired, fill in the background between the design and the outline with tiny stippling.

Trim and Mount

1. Remove the marking lines by submerging the quilted piece in cold water. Lay it flat to dry.

2. Working from the back side of the project, center the mat opening over the quilted design. Mark a line to be used as a guide for cutting away the excess batting and backing layers.

3. Trim away the unwanted layers. Leave only the top layer.

4. Trim the top layer 1½" beyond the quilted outlines.

5. Center the quilted piece on the square of mat board for mounting. Securely tape the edge down using the acid-free mounting tape.

Frame

1. Press the fabric that will cover the mat.

2. Position that fabric where you want the design to fit on the mat.

3. Mark the outline and opening of the mat on the back side of the fabric.

10. If desired, use thick tacky glue to attach the cording to the inside opening of the fabric that is secured to the face of the mat. Work around the edge, pressing the cording securely as you go.

4. Following the manufacturer's instructions, use the spray adhesive to lightly coat the front of the mat.

5. When the adhesive becomes tacky, position the fabric on it. Be sure to match up the outline with the mat edge.

6. Set the pieces aside to dry.

7. When the mat is dry, trim away the excess fabric from outer edge.

8. Make an X in the center opening of the mat using the sharp razor blade knife. Start with the blade in a corner and draw it toward the center of the opening.

9. Trim the triangles, making ¾" tabs that can be wrapped to the back side of the mat and taped securely with the acid-free tape.

11. Clip the flange of the cording at each corner.

12. Join the ends in a corner.

13. Insert the mat and the quilted design into the frame opening.

14. Close the back of the frame.

Classic Tiles Coasters, 4½" x 4½".

Stitch up a set of these elegant coasters to create the perfect little accent for your décor. Choose your favorite color of sateen, and load the machine with lightweight thread. You will have a beautiful set of coasters stitched before you know it. Trim them with matching binding, or try making a set using a contrasting solid or print fabric.

The coasters are small, and individually cut shapes may be difficult to hold onto during the quilting process. To make your work easier, leave the coasters attached in one large piece; trim them to the correct size after the quilting is completed.

materials

fabric

- ⅓ yd. solid fabric for top, backing and bias binding

notions

- ¼ yd. lightweight batting

- Lightweight thread to match the fabric

Cut

1. Cut two 6" x 24" pieces from the solid-colored fabric.

2. Cut one 6" x 24" piece of lightweight batting.

3. Cut four 1¼" x 20" strips to make the single-fold bias binding.

Mark

1. Copy the Classic Coaster pattern from the paper pullout. Because this design is so intricate, you may wish to use the alternate marking method described in Basic Techniques.

2. Tape the patterns to a hard surface, or light box if necessary.

3. Fold the solid fabric in half and then in half again to create four 6" sections.

4. Gently crease the fabric on the folds.

5. Center one square of the fabric over one pattern design.

6. Trace the pattern outlines.

7. Repeat Steps 5 and 6 until all of the squares are filled.

Quilt

1. Assemble the layers for quilting. See Basic Techniques for instructions.

2. Set up the sewing machine to use lightweight thread to match the color of the fabric.

3. Study the quilting sequence for the Classic Tiles Table Mat project. Complete a practice sample to familiarize yourself with the pattern and to ensure your machine's settings are correct. Refer to Basic Techniques for additional information.

4. Stitch each design.

5. If desired, fill in the background with tiny stippling. Make sure you fill the space to the outline of the squares.

Finish

1. When quilting is complete, submerge the piece in cold water to remove markings. Lay the piece flat to dry.

2. Trim the piece into 4½" squares.

3. Attach the bias binding. Refer to Finishing Touches for details on single-fold bias binding.

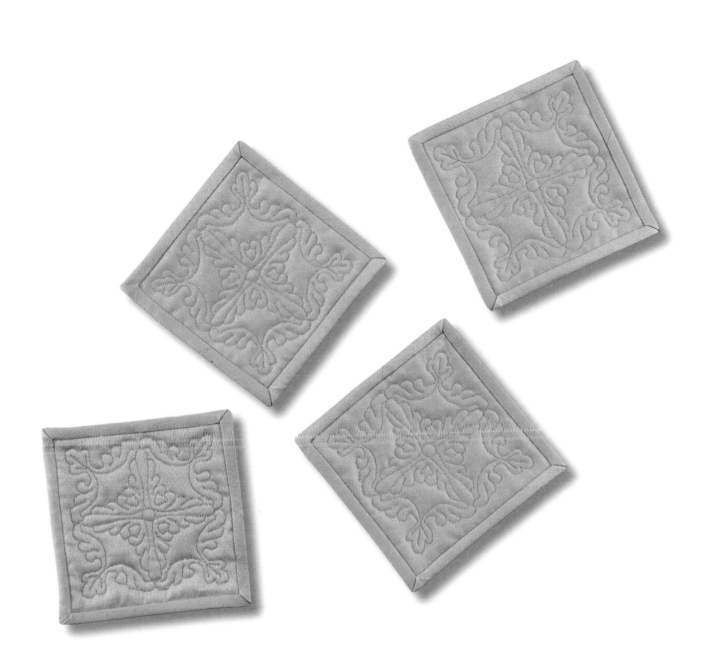

Classic Tiles Long Table Runner

Classic Tiles Long Table Runner, 12½" x 43".

The same design used for Classic Tiles Pillow Three has been developed into this practical table runner. Use your large-scale print and two solid fabrics as another accent for the decor of your room. Add a beaded tassel to finish the ends with pizazz.

materials

fabric

- ⅓ yd. solid fabric for points
- ½ yd. print fabric
- ⅓ yd. black fabric for bias binding
- ½ yd. backing fabric

notions

- ½ yd. batting
- Lightweight thread to match solid fabric
- Black thread
- 2 beads, any size (optional)
- 2 tassels, any size (optional)

Cut

1. Cut one 13" x 27" piece from the print fabric.

2. Use the Classic Tiles Long Table Runner pattern in the pullout section of the book as a template to cut out two pointed ends of the mat from the solid fabric.

3. Cut enough 2¼" wide bias strips to make 110" of binding from the black fabric.

4. Cut a 13" x 43" piece from the backing fabric.

5. Cut a 13" x 43" piece from the batting.

Assemble and Mark

1. Sew the two triangle ends to the print fabric.

2. Press the seams open.

3. Tape the Classic Tiles Triangle pattern to a hard surface, or light box if necessary.

4. Gently crease a fold in the center of the solid fabric.

5. Position the fabric over the paper design. Tape it in place.

6. Trace the outlines of the design onto the fabric. For the runner shown in the photo, every other line above the bud design was eliminated to simplify the quilting for this project.

Quilt

1. Assemble the layers for quilting. Refer to Basic Techniques for details.

2. Quilt the design using lightweight thread to match the solid fabric. Follow the quilting sequence given in the Classic Tiles Pillow Two project.

3. For the border quilting, follow the lines across the space and retrace any area necessary to continue along the design.

4. Use invisible thread to outline the flowers and leaves of the print fabric. Be sure to stitch all the way to the outer edges of the runner.

Finish

1. When quilting is complete, remove the markings by submerging the piece in cold water. Lay the piece flat to dry.

2. Place the quilted piece on a cutting mat, and trim it to 12½" wide. Leave ¼" outside the quilted outline around the points at the ends.

3. Assemble the binding strips. Apply them to the runner, following the instructions for binding in Finishing Touches.

4. Hand stitch the binding to the back side of the piece.

5. Sew one bead and one tassel to the point at each end.

Long Table Runner 121

Classic Tiles Wall Quilt, 36" x 36".

Classic Tiles

This wall quilt is the culmination of fabrics and designs in a room decorated with the Classic Tiles quilting theme. The project combines a large-scale print and several coordinating solid fabrics with the Classic Tiles quilting designs. Hang your quilt in an entryway or above a sofa full of coordinating pillows. Simple construction techniques guide you in making this focal point of the grouping.

materials

fabric

- ½ yd. black fabric for center panel of the top and binding
- 1¼ yd. print fabric for triangles and borders
- ¼ yd. green fabric for narrow border
- ¼ yd. light-colored fabric for corner blocks
- ⅔ yd. the copper-colored sateen for wide strips
- 1¼ yd. any fabric for backing

notions

- 45" x 60" batting
- Lightweight threads to match fabrics
- Invisible thread for quilting the print fabric
- Black thread

Cut

1. Cut one 14" x 14" piece from the solid fabric for the center panel. The project shown uses black.

2. Cut two 10" x 10" squares from the print fabric, then cut each square once on the diagonal to yield four triangles. The outside edges will have the straight grain, and the bias edge will be attached to the center square.

3. Cut eight 1¼" x 19½" narrow border strips from the green fabric.

4. Cut four 4" x 19¼" wide border strips from the copper-colored fabric. If sateen is used, cut two strips in each direction, and mark the top edges.

5. Cut four 5½" x 5½" blocks from the light-colored fabric for the corners. Mark the tops of the fabric if sateen is used.

6. Cut four 5" x 40" strips from print fabric for outer border. Pay attention to the print, and try to find an area that shows off the fabric best.

7. Cut one 40" x 40" piece from the backing fabric .

8. Cut one 40" x 40" piece from the batting.

9. Cut enough 2¼" wide strips to make 154" of double-fold bias binding from the solid black fabric.

Assemble

1. Sew two of the side triangles to opposite sides of the center square. Press the seams open.

2. Sew on the other two triangles to the square. Press the seams open.

3. Sew the inner borders of strip sets and corner blocks. Sew a narrow strip to each side of the four wide strips. Press the seams open.

4. Sew a corner block to each end of two of the assembled strips that will be for the top and bottom pieces.

tip

This large wall quilt has the "square within a square" quilt block for the central design, with several borders added. If you haven't sewn this block before, you may wonder how to attach the triangles to end up with a perfect square in the center and the accurate ¼" seam allowance needed when attaching the border. Here's a trick to use: cut the triangles ½" larger than the pattern states. Finger-press a crease in the center of one side of the square and the center of the longest side of the triangle. Match the creases. Pin the edges together. Repeat for the opposing side of the square. Sew the pieces to the square. Press the seams open. Add the other two triangles in the same manner, setting the inner square "on point" to complete the block. Next, lay the block on a large cutting mat to trim it into an accurate square. Align the ¼" line of the ruler on the intersection of he square and triangles, creating the seam allowance. The additional fabric added when cutting the triangles will ensure that you will keep the point of the inner square when the borders are added.

5. Press the seams away from the corner block.

6. Sew a set of border strips, without the corner blocks, to the sides of the center of the quilt. Press the seams away from the center.

7. Sew the other set of border strips to the top and bottom of the quilt. The intersecting seams where the side borders meet the corner blocks should lock. Press the seams away from the center of the quilt.

8. Sew two of the pieces of the wide border to the sides of the quilt. Stop ¼" from the corner. Press the seams open.

9. Sew the final two wide border strips, stopping ¼" from the corner. Press the seams open.

10. Fold the quilt center on the diagonal to allow the borders to be marked and trimmed for the 90-degree miter.

11. Sew the miter for each corner.

12. Press the seams open.

Mark

1. Copy the Classic Tiles Wall Quilt pattern from the pullout pattern.

2. Tape it to a hard surface, or light box if necessary, or use a white marker.

3. Trace the quilting lines onto the fabric.

Quilt

1. Assemble the layers for quilting. Refer to Basic Techniques for details.

2. Follow the quilting sequence from Classic Tiles Pillow One for the center and corner blocks.

3. Use invisible thread to anchor the layers together along the center square, outer border and corner blocks.

4. Use black thread to quilt the center designs.

5. Use invisible thread to quilt the flowers and leaves of the printed triangles.

6. Use copper-colored thread to outline the copper-colored border strips, to quilt the designs and to do the stippling. Follow the border design lines, retracing any area of the line necessary to continue to the area that needs to be stitched next.

7. Use light-colored thread to outline the corner blocks, stitch the designs and fill in the stippling.

8. Use invisible thread to quilt the flowers and leaves of the printed outer borders.

tip

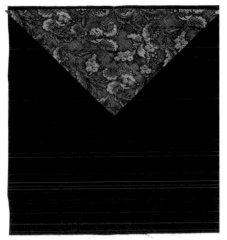

Here's a trick to sew the triangles to the square to make a perfect center block. Cut the squares from which you will cut the triangles ½" larger than the pattern states. Finger press a crease in the center of each side of the center square and the longest side of each triangle. Match the creases.

Sew the triangle to one side, and then sew on the opposing side. Press the seams open. Add the other two sides, then press the seams open. Lay the assembled piece on a cutting mat and trim it with the 1/4" line of the ruler just outside of the point where the triangles meet the corner of the square. You will not lose the point of the square when the borders are added.

Finish

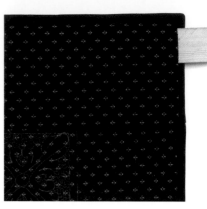

1. When quilting is complete, wet the entire piece with cold water to remove markings.

2. Lay the piece flat to dry.

3. Square up the dry piece by laying it on a cutting mat.

4. Trim the piece to a 36" square.

5. If you plan to hang the quilt, add the rod pocket. See Finishing Touches for more details about rod pockets.

6. Attach the bias binding; refer to Finishing Touches for details.

Classic Tiles Pincushion and Strawberry Emery Bags

Classic Tiles Pincushion, 4¼" x 4¼", and coordinating Strawberry Emery Bags.

Here are some adorable little sewing companions. They will make a sweet treat for your eyes whenever you sew, or they could make a thoughtful gift for a friend who stitches.

Each strawberry begins with a manufactured emery bag for the base that is covered with fancy fabric and embellished. The pincushion is a miniature version of the Pillow with Cording described in Finishing Touches. It uses the same quilting design as the Classic Tiles Coasters. Wool is a great choice for filling a pincushion, and you can use up your wool batting leftovers for this project. Shred the scraps and use them to stuff the pincushion.

---

materials (for one pincushion)

fabric

- ¼ yd. sateen fabric for top, backing and cording
- 8" x 8" scrap of fabric for pincushion lining, which won't be seen

notions

- 8" x 8" scrap of batting
- Polyester or wool stuffing
- Lightweight thread to match fabric
- ½ yd. lightweight cord to make your own cording, or ½ yd. small-scale manufactured cording (optional)

tools and supplies

- Zipper foot for sewing machine

Cut

1. Cut an 8" x 8" piece from the sateen for the cushion top.

2. Cut an 8" x 8" scrap of fabric for the lining.

3. Cut an 8" x 8" piece from the sateen for the backing fabric.

4. Cut an 8" x 8" piece from the batting.

5. If you are making your own cording, cut a 1½" x 20" bias strip from the sateen.

Mark

1. Copy the Classic Tiles Coaster pattern from the paper pullout from the back of the book.

2. Tape the pattern to a hard surface, or light box if necessary. You also can use the alternate marking method explained in Basic Techniques.

3. Center the fabric square over the paper design.

4. Trace the design on the fabric.

Quilt

1. Assemble the layers for quilting. Refer to Basic Techniques for more information.

2. Study the quilting sequence for the Classic Tiles Table Mat Project. Complete a practice sample to familiarize yourself with the pattern and ensure your machine's settings are correct.

3. Quilt the designs using thread that matches the fabric.

4. If desired, add tiny stippling in the empty spaces in the background of the pincushion.

Finish

1. When quilting is complete, submerge the piece in cold water to remove the markings. Lay the piece flat to dry.

2. Trim the dry quilted piece to a 4¼" square.

3. Using the zipper foot, add the cording to the edge of the square. See Finishing Touches for directions on how to make your own cording.

4. Assemble the pincushion using the instructions for a Pillow with Cording found in Finishing Touches.

Strawberry Emery Bags

Inexpensive manufactured emery bags were covered for this little sewing room accent. This pattern will fit an emery bag that is 2¼" long and 1" wide at the top. Other manufactured emery bags may be sized a bit differently; adjust the pattern as needed to fit the bags.

One bag is covered with a classically woven silk fabric in a rich bronze color. DMC No. 5 Perle Cotton was used to stitch a strawberry leaf pattern and make a twisted hanging loop. The other bag is covered in deep teal sateen, embellished with amber glass beads and topped off with a fabric yo-yo.

materials (for two emery bags)

fabric

- Fancy fabric scraps in silk brocade and sateen

notions

- Thread to match fabric
- 2 strawberry-shaped manufactured emery bags
- Amber glass iridescent beads
- DMC No. 5 Perle Cotton

tools and supplies

- Thick white glue
- Beading needle

Emery bag history

In the days when a needle was a treasured possession as well as an essential household tool, fancy needle cases and pincushions were used to hold needles for safekeeping.

Many pincushions had a little strawberry-shaped bag attached, filled with emery, a polishing compound used to keep the needle polished and sharp.

Cut and Assemble

1. Cut two 4½" squares from the fabric scraps.

2. Sew two adjacent sides of the square together to form a cone shape.

3. Slip the emery bag inside the cone.

4. Adjust the seam until it fits the emery bag snugly.

5. Trim off the excess top fabric.

6. Glue the edges to conform to the shape of the strawberry. Use as little glue as possible.

7. Repeat Steps 2 through 6 for the second emery bag.

Finish

Beaded Emery Bag

1. Sew tiny beads in even rows spaced about ¼" apart on the entire surface of the unembellished emery bag.

2. Cut a 2" circle from the sateen fabric to make a yo-yo to finish the top of the emery bag.

3. Sew a running stitch around the raw edge of the sateen circle. Gather the running stitch tightly. Knot the thread.

4. Cut a 6" piece of the perle cotton and fold it in half. Twist the perle cotton to form a 3" stem.

5. Glue the perle cotton to the center of the yo-yo.

6. Glue the yo-yo to the top of the emery bag.

Silk Strawberry Emery Bag

1. Cover the emery bag with silk brocade fabric as described in the Assemble steps.

2. Use long stitches, made with the perle cotton, to form a five-pointed leaf pattern that covers the raw edges of the fabric at the top of the bag.

3. Add the stem in the same manner described for the beaded emery bag.

Classic Tiles
Variations

So many ideas evolved when I was thinking of options to use elements of the Classic Tiles designs in different projects. Here are a few ideas for you to try.

Classic Tiles Tablecloth

Some variations are as simple as coming up with an additional use for an existing project. The Classic Tiles Wall Quilt easily does double-duty as a tablecloth for a small table.

More Classic Tiles Pillows

Make a pair of large floor pillows using any of the Classic Tiles Pillow patterns. Use the chart in Basic Techniques to increase the size of the pattern.

Try other pillow shapes, such as neck rolls or rectangular pillows, using the Classic Tiles patterns. Your imagination is the only limit to how these designs could be used.

Classic Tiles Place Mats

Reduce the size of the Classic Tiles Table Mat to make a set of matching place mats. Set the copy machine at 75 percent to adjust the design so it works for 12" x 18" place mats.

Classic Tiles Patchwork Accents

Try the Classic Tiles Pillows One and Two designs to fill the empty blocks of other patchwork projects you may have.

Decorative embellishments are the icing on the cake. This chapter features easy techniques to add finishing touches to the projects in the book. Paint your own lace to coordinate with any decor by blending the colors of your fabrics and wallpaper. Follow the simple guidelines for making and attaching binding, making your own cording and finishing pillows. Impress your friends with your new skills.

Finishing Touches

For the Love of Trim

I absolutely love lace and trim — possibly even more than my fabric stash. I love to poke around in the trim department of a fabric store and discover the treasures waiting there. Just holding it in my hands causes my imagination to run wild. I become inspired to rush right home to create a project that I can embellish with my pretty new delights.

Our sons both are in school in Chicago, which is about a three-hour drive from our home. It is worth giving up a day of sewing just to go to Vogue Fabrics and see what is new. If I travel to a city that has a fabric district, I am in heaven on Earth. The more bins to pick through, the better the adventure. I hope that you will be inspired to begin a collection of wonderful embellishments that could be used for these projects, or, you may use some of the treasures you already have in your stash.

I use trim sparingly on the projects in this book, choosing a few tasteful accents to showcase the luscious fabrics. You can choose from the many beautiful selections available and use as much or as little as you wish.

Hand-Painted Lace

When choosing lace, the size of one individual motif will impact the finished size of the quilted piece. Lace with smaller motifs is easier to work with for these projects. Large increments may require you to adjust the pattern to fit the lace properly.

Experiment with a variety of paints manufactured for fabric. Choose a color that matches your fabric and one or more that accent the project. Regular acrylic paints can be used when mixed with a fabric medium; follow the manufacturer's directions. Pre-shrink the lace before painting it; you don't want to cut to the finished length and have it end up too small.

materials

- Flat lace in rayon or cotton/rayon blend
- Water-based acrylic fabric paint
- Acrylic paint to match your fabric
- Acrylic paint to serve as an accent color
- Fabric medium
- Paintbrush
- Dropcloth to protect the painting surface
- Water
- Bowl
- Hair dryer or iron and ironing board
- White paper towels

Paint

1. Thin the paint with water until it reaches the consistency of ink.

2. Lay the lace out flat on top of the dropcloth.

3. Paint two-thirds of the lace motif with one color of paint. If you want the colors to remain more distinct, let it dry. To get colors to blend into one another, go to Step 4.

4. Paint the other third of the lace motif with the darker paint. Blend the deeper colors where they overlap. It may take several coats of paint to get the intensity you desire.

5. Let the paint air dry, or you can dry it quickly using a hair dryer or iron. If you use an iron, protect the wet lace with layers of white paper towels.

6. Heat set the paint according to the manufacturer's instructions.

Handmade Cording

It takes a little time, but you can make your own cording right at home, saving time and money by using what you already have on hand. Making your own cording is easy to do, and it will perfectly match your project. Cording made from matching fabric was used for the Classic Tiles Pincushion. It also could be used instead of manufactured cording for other projects.

Before you start making cording, read the information on pages 142–143 about binding and bias strips to familiarize yourself with the process.

materials

- ⅛" wide to ½" wide uncovered cord from a drapery department (soft is better than stiff)

- Fabric bias strips cut 1" wide for tiny cording or 1¾" wide for larger cording

- Thread to match the fabric

- Sewing machine

- Zipper foot for the sewing machine

- Iron and ironing board

- Measuring tape

- Scissors

Make the Cording

1. Measure around your project to determine how much cording you need. Add a few extra inches to allow for overlapping ends.

2. Cut enough bias strips to make the needed length of fabric when sewn into one piece.

3. Sew the bias strips together.

4. Press the seams open.

5. Fold the bias strip in half lengthwise, right side out.

6. Insert the cord into the fold of the bias strip.

7. Attach the zipper foot to your machine. Move the needle position all the way to the left.

8. Using a medium stitch length, stitch the entire length of the piece as close to the cording as possible.

Attach the Cording

1. Pin the cording to the project, starting at the least obvious place on the item. Match the raw edges of the cording with the raw edge of the project.

2. Clip the cording flange at the corners, and round them slightly.

3. Sew around the edge until you get to the final side. Stop stitching 6" away from the beginning end.

4. To join the ends, remove a few stitches to expose the cord. Line up the cord ends next to one another and cut through both of them so that they butt each other.

5. Replace the fabric around the cord on one end, and trim it the same length as the cord.

6. Cut the fabric on the other end 1" longer than the overlap.

7. Fold the raw edge under. Wrap it around the other cord.

8. Continue the line of stitching to complete the entire edge.

Pillow Finishing Techniques

Pillow With Two-Panel Back Closure

With the two-panel back, a pillow does not need to be sewn closed after the pillow form is inserted. It is constructed inside out; the cording is applied first, and the back pieces are applied in a second step. The two overlapping back panels allow the pillow form to easily be inserted and removed.

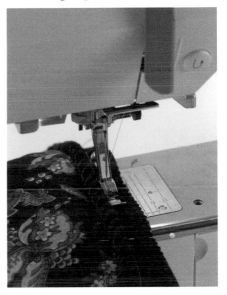

materials

- Quilted pillow top
- Backing fabric, with measurements based on size of the quilted pillow top
- Pillow form to fit finished pillow top
- Sewing thread to match cording
- Sewing machine with zipper foot
- Manufactured or homemade cording
- Iron
- Ironing board
- Fusible web (optional)
- Scissors
- Pins

Measure and Cut

1. Measure the front fabric or quilted pillow top. The back will be the same measurement when the two halves are overlapped.

2. Cut two back panels from the backing fabric. Each panel should measure the height of the pillow by half the width of the pillow back plus 4".

Sew

1. Starting at the bottom center of the pillow, pin the flange or selvage edge of the cording to the raw edge of the pillow front. Round the corners slightly, and snip the selvage of the cording at the corners to allow it to expand and lay flat.

2. Join the two ends of cording by overlapping them at the beginning point.

3. Attach the zipper foot to your sewing machine. Move the needle position all the way to the left.

4. Stitch the trim onto the pillow. Go around the entire edge of the pillow, and stitch as close to the cording as possible.

5. Press a 1" hem onto the center edge of each of the pillow backing pieces.

6. Secure the hem by stitching the edge with matching thread or fusing it with a strip of fusible web.

7. Pin one piece of the backing to the pillow front. Position right sides together and match raw edges.

8. Position the other piece of the backing fabric, overlapping the first side. Pin it in place.

9. Using the zipper foot, stitch around the entire edge.

10. Trim the edges, if needed, and turn the pillow right side out.

11. Stuff the pillow form into the case, and adjust it to fill the corners.

materials

- Quilted pillow top
- Fabric for bias strips
- Fabric for pillow back
- 1" wide strip of batting that is the same length as the binding
- Thread to match cording
- Sewing machine with zipper foot
- Walking foot for sewing machine (optional)
- Pillow form to fit top

Cut

1. Square up the pillow top according to pattern instructions.

2. Cut the pillow back and an extra layer of batting to the same size as the top.

3. From the binding fabric, cut 2½" wide bias strips totaling the length needed.

Sew

1. Sew the bias strips together to make one long piece. Press the bias strip seams open.

Pillow with Faux Cording

Faux cording is quilt binding that is stuffed. Pillows that use this technique appear as though cording has been sewn into the seam. However, this method is much easier to apply than regular cording. No zippers or overlapping backs are needed.

With this method, a wide binding stuffed with batting is applied to the front and back layers, just like binding would be added to a quilt. Since the pillow is layered with the right sides of the fabric out, no turning is necessary. An extra layer of batting added to the pillow back makes the pillow smooth and free of gaps.

2. Fold the bias strip in half lengthwise, with wrong sides together. Press.

3. Press under one end of the bias strip by ¼".

4. Insert a 1" wide strip of batting between the layers of the folded binding.

5. Refer to the instructions in this chapter for adding binding to a quilt. Follow the procedure given for the corners and joining of the ends.

6. Add the binding to the entire edge of the pillow front. Start with the turned-under end at the bottom center of the pillow and continue until you overlap the ends. If you have a walking foot for your machine, use it to help keep the layers even.

7. Lay the pillow back right side down.

8. Place a layer of batting on top of the pillow back.

9. Place the pillow top right side up on top of the batting and backing layers. Match the raw edges.

10. Pin the three layers together, leaving an 8" opening for stuffing at the bottom of the pillow.

11. Sew the layers together on the same line of stitching used to attach the binding. Backstitch at the pins, and leave the opening unsewn.

12. Stuff the pillow form into the pillow.

13. Continue the line of machine stitching to sew the opening closed.

14. Turn the binding over pillow edge. Pin evenly.

15. Slipstitch the folded edge to the back of the pillow.

materials

- Large cutting mat
- 24" ruler
- An extra ruler, which can be smaller
- Rotary cutter

Sizing the Finished Quilt Top

When the quilting is completed, the markings are removed and the quilt is dry, it is time to square up the quilt top. The process described here will help you to trim the quilt accurately, even when the lines of the mat can't be seen.

Cut

1. Lay the quilted piece on a cutting mat. Position the quilt so that one side is on a line at the bottom of the mat.

2. Align the outside edge of the right border with a line on the right side of the mat.

3. Place the 24" ruler along the outside edge of the right border of the quilt.

4. Measure the distance from the right edge of the 24" ruler to the edge of the mat.

5. Use the second ruler to make sure that the 24" ruler is on the line that is cover from sight by the quilt.

6. Trim the piece through all layers along the ruler edge.

7. Rotate the piece clockwise to the next size. Repeat Steps 2 through 6 until all of the sides are trimmed.

Rod Pockets

A hanging sleeve or rod pocket is used to slip a dowel through to hang a quilt on a wall. The tube of fabric is attached to the top edge of the backside of the quilt. The sleeve can be added to a finished quilt by hand stitching both edges to the quilt. Or follow these steps and sew the first edge by machine when adding the binding.

materials

- Fabric
- Thread to match the fabric
- Dowel
- Ironing board and iron
- Sewing machine
- Fusible web (optional)

Cut and Press

1. Cut a strip of fabric that measures 9" tall by the width of the quilt plus 1". Fold under ½" of each 9" end. Press.

2. Repeat Step 1 for the other side of the pocket so the sleeve is 1" shorter than the quilt's width.

Sew and Fuse

1. Fold the strip in half lengthwise. Sew the fold to hold it permanently. Or slip a ½" wide strip of fusible web into the fold and fuse it to hold it permanently.

2. Using a ¼" seam allowance and a walking foot, sew the raw edges of the sleeve to the top edge of the quilt. Match raw edges and center the sleeve on the quilt.

3. Follow the instructions for attaching the binding on pages 142-143.

4. Pin the folded edge of the sleeve to the quilt, allowing it to bulge out to give extra space for the thickness of the rod.

5. Slip stitch the edge securely. Take care to catch only the backing so that the stitches are not seen on the front of the quilt.

materials

- Fabric
- Cutting mat
- Rotary cutter
- Thread to match the fabric
- Sewing machine with walking foot
- Iron and ironing board
- Spray starch

Cut

1. Line up the bottom edge of the fabric with the bottom edge of the cutting mat.

2. Place the ruler across the fabric on the 45-degree angle line of the mat.

3. Trim off the corner of the fabric on that line. Set the fabric triangle aside.

Binding

Most of the binding used for the projects in this book is bias-cut fabric strips that are cut 2¼" wide. Use bias-cut strips that are folded in half to double the thickness of the fabric, which will give a full-bodied, long-wearing edge. The coaster projects use a single-fold bias binding that is cut 1¼" wide.

Instructions are given to join the ends of the binding with a simple overlapping method. There are other, more complicated methods to join the ends. Use any technique with which you are comfortable.

Always start by stabilizing the fabric. Press it using spray starch to avoid stretching the bias strips before you cut them.

4. Rotate the newly cut edge to line up with the 0-line on the left side of the mat.

5. Place the ruler on top of the fabric. Line up the 2¼" mark on the ruler with the cut edge of the fabric. If the fabric you started with is larger than the cutting mat, fold it in half and match the cut edge.

6. Cut enough 2¼" wide fabric strips to total the length needed for the project.

Sew

1. Lay the strips out flat with all of the right sides up.

2. Position the strips with the ends at the same diagonal cut.

3. With one strip right side up, flip the second strip to be added on top at a right angle to the bottom strip. Match the raw edges. You will know the fabric is positioned correctly if a triangle of fabric sticks out at each end.

4. Using a ¼" seam allowance, sew the pieces together with a line of stitching that begins and ends at the little triangles.

5. Sew all of the strips together in this manner to make one long piece.

Press

1. Press each seam open.

2. Fold the binding in half lengthwise with the wrong sides of fabric together.

3. Press the binding. Add spray starch to prevent stretching during application.

Apply the Binding

1. Turn one end of the binding strip under by ¼".

2. Choose the most inconspicuous place on the project to have the binding ends join.

3. Place the folded end of the binding strip at that place, and line up the raw edge of the binding with the raw edge of the quilt.

4. Pin the layers together to keep the edges even, but only along the first edge.

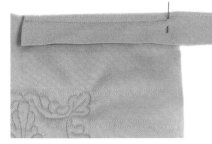

5. Place a pin ¼" before the edge of the project. This will mark the point at which you will stop stitching.

6. Use the walking foot for your sewing machine to hold all the layers together evenly as you sew. Stitch through all layers ¼" from raw edge, stopping ¼" from corner. Backstitch, lift the needle out of the fabric, and clip the threads.

7. To form a mitered corner, fold the binding strip upward at a 90-degree angle, then fold it back down, lining up the raw edge with the second side.

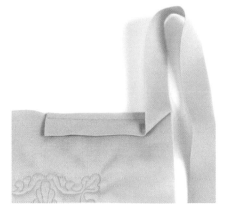

8. Begin sewing at the edge of the strip, and stop ¼" before the next corner. Continue sewing all sides in this manner.

9. To join the two ends of the strip, overlap the strip on the final side, ½" past the starting place. Stop the line of stitching, then backstitch and trim off any excess length.

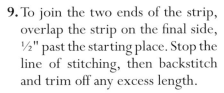

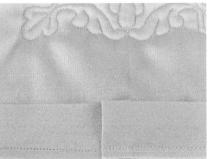

10. Fold the binding over the quilt edge and cover all of the raw edges.

11. Pin or clip the binding evenly along the backside of the quilt, and slip stitch the folded edge securely.

✂ Single-Fold Binding

This lightweight version of bias binding is scaled for use with smaller coaster projects. The strips should be cut long enough to avoid the need to seam pieces together.

1. Cut strips 1¼" wide.

2. Sew unfolded strips to the projects.

3. Follow the remaining steps outlined for double-fold binding to finishe the piece.

Resources

Tools

Bernina Sewing Machine
Hans' Sewing and Vacuum
1525 Williamson St.
Madison, WI 53703
(800) 739-8221
e-mail: info@sewvac1.com
http://www.sewvac1.com

EZ Snips
Specialty Scissors Sales
15155 Bailey Hill Road
Brooksville, FL 34614
(352) 797-9057
e-mail: mrscissors@yahoo.com

The Free-Motion Slider
LaPierre Studio LLC
e-mail: Quiltpack@aol.com

Matting and Framing
Mad Matter
N.R. Potter
5068 Hardy Trail
Waunakee, WI 53597

Notions
Golden Thread Quilting Paper
Golden Threads
2 S 373 Seneca Drive
Wheaton, IL 60187
(888) 477-7718
e-mail: info@goldenthreads.com
http://www.goldenthreads.com

Hobbs Heirloom Wool Batting
Hobbs Bonded Fibers
Craft Products Division
P.O. Box 2521
Waco, TX 76702-2521
(800) 433-3357
http://www.hobbsbondedfibers.com

Insul-Bright Insulated Lining
The Warm Company
954 E. Union St.
Seattle, WA 98122
(800) 234-WARM
e-mail: info@warmcompany.com
http://www.warmcompany.com

The Bottom Line™ Superior Threads
P.O. Box 1672
St. George, UT 84771
(800) 499-1777
e-mail: info@superiorthreads.com
http://www.superiorthreads.com

YLI Silk and Invisible Thread
YLI Corporation
161 West Main St.
Rock Hill, SC 29730
(803) 985-3100
e-mail: ylicorp@ylicorp.com
http://www.ylicorpo.com

Fabric
Sateen Fabrics
RJR Fabrics
2203 Dominguez St., Building K-3
Torrance, CA 90501
(800) 422-5426
e-mail: info@rjrfabrics.com
http://www.rjrfabrics.com

Recommended Reading

"Elegant Machine Quilting" is a book of designs and projects. It is not intended to be a comprehensive guide to heirloom machine quilting, but an overview of the basic procedures to follow to complete these projects. I strongly recommend the following books:

- "Guide to Machine Quilting," by Diane Gaudynski;
- "Heirloom Machine Quilting," by Harriet Hargrave;
- "Trapunto by Machine," by Hari Walner; and
- "Pathways to Better Quilting," by Sally Terry.